CATS' COMPANY

" Siamese kittens don't go to school, you silly little thing."

CATS' COMPANY

by Compton Mackenzie

Taplinger Publishing Co., Inc.,
New York

Published in the United States by
Taplinger Publishing Co., Inc., 1961

Library of Congress Catalog Card Number 61-13515

Originally published in Great Britain
by Elek Books Ltd., London.

PRINTED IN GREAT BRITAIN

Contents

To Elsa, the Queen of Cats,
with profound respect.

All the photographs in this book, with the exception of the two facing page 73 which are reproduced by permission of Sir Compton Mackenzie, were specially taken by G. Harrison Marks.

" I hope it's all right being photographed with this tabby."

" Did you think I was a lion cub? "

Mr. Barnes and Snow

In the Spring of 1885 when I was just two years old a small house had been taken by my parents in Malvern where my younger brother was to be born that May. It was there that my lifelong devotion to cats began. He was a very large neuter tabby, and as I look back at him from nearly 75 years ago he seems almost the size of a lion. The landlady's name was Barnes and being a widow without any Mr. Barnes about the place I called her cat "Mr. Barnes".

Two aunts were staying in Malvern, each with a fox-terrier puppy, Scamp and Ranx. The latter was given this odd name for a dog because the aunt to whom he belonged had been playing the heroine in a melodrama by G. R. Sims and Henry Pettit called *In The Ranks* which had recently enjoyed a run of eighteen months at the Adelphi Theatre.

Mr. Barnes used to warn me that if I encouraged these two puppies I might find their boisterous attentions more than I could cope with, but I never could resist calling "Baby bow-bows" and I would then have somehow to maintain myself on my feet while Scamp who was spotted with brown and Ranx who was all white jumped up and licked my face. "Go down, baby bow-wows," I used to plead, and Mr. Barnes would shake his head.

"I can do nothing for you," his disapproving green eyes would say. "I warned you not to encourage them. They'll knock you over one of these days."

It must have been Mr. Barnes who convinced me all those years ago that fond as I was of dogs the cat was a more civilized creature, friendship with whom was a privilege less easily gained than friendship with a dog. Somebody once said that a dog looked up to a man as its superior, that a horse regarded a man as its equal and that a cat looked down on him as its inferior. Scamp and Ranx undoubtedly looked upon me as an equal. Mr. Barnes never did that, but his superiority

7

was always expressed in the kindliest way and he never had to censure me for handling him clumsily or trying to make him do something he did not want to do.

My first animal love had been a Skye terrier called Laddie. When my mother married she had given Laddie away to her sister because my father, devoted to horses, was embarrassed by dogs as some people are by children. Laddie never forgave her and when she went to see her sister he would immediately retire under a sofa and refuse to speak to her. However, he was always friendly with myself. Indeed, he and I had been photographed together not long before that time at Malvern, but on the very next day he had been stolen, and was never seen by any of us again. Hence the acquisition of the obstreperous Ranx who lived on to a fat and lazy old age.

Mr. Barnes encouraged me with my reading. We used to sit under a laburnum tree when the weather, which had been horribly cold that April, grew warmer while I read him the story of Dick Whittington. My mother had been rather discouraging about having Dick Whittington read to her because there was a double-page coloured picture of the rats eating everything up and being in what Victorian politeness used to call an 'interesting condition', she had thought that this picture, which I continually pressed upon her attention, might have a disastrous effect upon the features of her unborn child. Mr. Barnes was naturally a sympathetic observer of this picture and did not mind how often I showed it to him. He also liked another double-page coloured picture of Tom Thumb on the verge of being swallowed by an enormous fish with two rows of savage teeth. As for myself I was so frightened of this picture that it required an effort of courage to turn the page and enjoy the ghastly fascination of it. Mr. Barnes used to reassure me. If this horrible fish took it into its head to emerge from the book and try to swallow me he knew how to deal with any fish. On one occasion he saved me from two blackbeetles which were walking across my cot: he did not succeed in catching them but he chased them out of the room and came back to lie at the foot of the cot until I fell asleep. The elderly Nanny who had been engaged to look after myself and the boy or girl who was to arrive always used to banish Mr. Barnes from my cot because he was credited with the intention of overlaying me as soon as I was asleep. The first of many battles with that old Nanny which would last for another five years was over "that great cat". Mr. Barnes also sympathized with my hostility to bluebottle flies. If a bluebottle came buzzing into the room

" There's no room for me."

" I'm just as sweet as the Siamese girl."

Mr. Barnes did not rest until he had caught it on the window-pane and, I am bound to add, eaten it.

We left Malvern in July and I never saw Mr. Barnes again, but I owe him much for teaching me before I was two-and-a-half to understand how cats hope that human beings will behave.

It could be repetitive and tedious if I were to spend time on recalling all the cats of my boyhood, but Snow deserves a page or two. She was a pure white half-Persian with one brilliant blue eye and an equally brilliant green one, and like so many white cats she was quite deaf.

On a wild March morning in 1897 I found a callow missel-thrush which had fallen from the nest and broken its leg. I took it home and managed to set the leg with a match. Before long Prush was hopping about and enjoying the freedom of the house both in Hampshire and in London. My brother and I took him to the country every Friday after school and brought him back to London on Sunday. Prush lived in a cage but he was usually out of it, and when it was time for him to go to bed he used to fly to the most inaccessible perch he could find in order to avoid being put to bed.

He was an incredibly intelligent bird and when he noticed that Snow's entry into the room was the signal for him to be put in his cage he decided that he must take every opportunity he could of scoring off Snow. He was so well able to look after himself that very soon we did not bother to catch him and put him in his cage. Now his delight was to wait until Snow was lying on the hearthrug in luxurious sleep and then fly down and peck her tail. He soon discovered that he could tease her even when she was awake because she was too deaf to hear him approach. Finally poor Snow was so much at his mercy that she used to rush out of the room when he arrived in it. We had a cook at that time who objected to her kitchen's being messed about by Prush and she used to wave a cloth at him to scare him away. So Prush decided to have his revenge on her. He found that he could pull plates out of the rack where they were drying, his pleasure in this being enhanced by the crash making Snow bolt out of the kitchen. He was not too popular with our parlour-maid either, because he used to hop into a tin of golden syrup and then leave treacly footprints all over the tablecloth in order to enjoy the pleasure of pecking at them and savouring the sweetness.

Prush was the most quick-witted bird I have known and I believe that but for a sad accident which cut short his life before he was a year old I could even have taught him to say a few words or two. He was near to achieving this when he died.

Prush loved teasing poor Snow but he became the playmate of Pat, an Airedale-Irish terrier and used to enjoy particularly a game in which Pat would lift his paw and pretend to defend himself from Prush's attacks. After the game was over Prush used to explore the kennel. One day when the game was going on Pat's paw came down heavily on Prush and broke his back: the poor dog was much distressed about the accident and came whining to tell me what had happened.

Twinkle

AFTER I went down from Oxford in June 1904 I lived in a delightful Elizabethan house at Burford called Ladyham, and later in that summer I brought back Twinkle from a village in Somerset where I had been staying. He was a Manx kitten, a beautifully marked tabby with a white shirtfront and white gloves, and when he came to live with me he was tiny enough to travel with comfort in a small birdcage. Twinkle was the only Manx cat I have known intimately, but when later on I first met Siamese cats I found that their behaviour and physique reminded me of Twinkle. I have wondered whether the origin of the Manx cat might be sought in the Malay jungle cat from which the Siamese cat is undoubtedly descended. The royal Siamese cats were semi-albinos and the result of exclusive breeding through some hundreds of years in order to provide a suitable animal to receive the souls of deceased members of the royal house if in their next transmigration they were to become animals. I noted in my diary for March 26th 1947, after arriving at Bangkok from Singapore in a Sunderland flying boat:

"We came down in the grey-green river and had tea while we were waiting for the luggage to come ashore. A ginger Siamese cat, not of the blood royal, miaowed in authentic Siamese and I gave her milk. At home a ginger female is rare. Her light green eyes were set Siamese fashion, her ears were large and her tail was kinked at the end. After she was fed she crouched beside my chair in typical Siamese attitude . . . I have little doubt we can assign the origin of the Manx cat to these Malay or Siamese common cats. The cross between a Siamese and Persian cat often results in taillessness, even when the Siamese sire or queen has a long unkinked tail. Moreover, this taillessness will persist through several generations.

11

Probably some sailor brought the cats back with him to the Isle of Man from an Eastern voyage."

Twinkle used to sleep at the foot of my bed, but when he began his amatory career he always spent the night out, returning at four o'clock every morning. He used to climb up an ancient espalier pear tree, one of two that grew against the front of the house, and jump from a bough on to the gutter above the window of my bedroom. Then from the gutter he would jump through the window open at the top in one leap on to my bed, and sleep where he was accustomed to sleep, at the foot of it. After the first two or three times his arrival very seldom disturbed me and for months I never failed to find him in his place by daylight. When his jump did wake me I used to strike a match to see the time; it was always exactly four o'clock.

Twinkle was convinced that he owned that pear-tree. I remember he once killed a pigeon and after decapitating it he pulled the dead bird between the trunk of the pear-tree and the wall of the house. Then for the rest of the day he sat on guard, growling whenever anybody except myself approached the tree.

There were three chairs in my library, two of them deep low wicker-chairs that undergraduates favoured in my time, the third a grandfather's chair. I used to sit in one of the wicker-chairs. Smut, a bulldog bitch, occupied the other, and the grandfather's chair was Twinkle's property. One evening before Twinkle came up from his supper I urged Smut to get up and lie in Twinkle's chair. She did not like the notion; she felt sure that Twinkle would resent her action, and for a time wriggling like a propitiatory spaniel she kept trying to get into her own chair. Finally I insisted on her getting into Twinkle's chair and there she lay, obviously embarrassed, unable to settle herself comfortably and looking at me with reproachful eyes that plainly begged me to let her retire to her own chair.

Then my housekeeper, followed by Twinkle, arrived with the coffee. The cat walked across to his own chair but stopped when he saw that it was occupied, and by a dog! Poor Smut's kinked tail tapped the seat of the chair in her agitation. She was obviously assuring Twinkle that she had not ventured to usurp his chair of her own accord; she had been made to occupy it by somebody who must not be disobeyed. Finally Smut could stand the strain of being stared at by this coldly arrogant Manx cat no longer. She jumped down and got into her own chair, with a look appealing to my better nature to let her stay there.

Twinkle advanced after Smut's retreat and I thought he was going to get up into his chair. Not at all. He contemptuously sniffed the edge of it; then turning his back on his own chair which had been profaned by a dog he retired under a low divan on the other side of the library and remained hidden from view for two hours. He then emerged and, his dudgeon alleviated, settled himself down on the divan which thence onward provided his evening siesta before midnight chimed the hour for love; he never got into the grandfather's chair again.

In the company of Twinkle and Smut I experienced the only inexplicable phenomenon I have encountered in my life. It was about nine o'clock of a breathless evening of heavy frost, and the moon was riding high in a cloudless sky of scintillating stars. Twinkle was sitting in the grandfather's chair (I had not yet played on him that practical joke) and Smut was in her wicker chair. Suddenly a soft sibilance began to whisper round the room at about the height of the door. Twinkle's eyes followed the sound, but Smut's ears were not pricked. I thought at first it must be a moth fluttering on the window-pane, but when I pulled the curtain there was nothing to be seen except the motionless orchard in the moonlight. My housekeeper was out visiting friends, but downstairs my gardener was studying seed catalogues in the kitchen, and I rang for him to come up and suggest an explanation for the strange sound. When he opened the door of my room the sound went past him out into the corridor, a faint sibilance upon the air.

"Did anything go past you when you opened the door?" I asked.

"Yes, something went singing past me down the passage like a kettle."

The gardener unhooked the reflector lamp from the wall, but we could see nothing. However, when we reached the end of the corridor which ran the length of the house we heard the sound again, moving back toward my library. We followed it, but instead of going into the library it went up a box-staircase that led to the great empty attic in the roof.

"Can it be a bat?" I asked.

"Queer kind of a bat," was the contemptuous reply. "Besides, we'd have seen a bat."

"Is it the wind?" I pressed.

"There isn't no wind to-night. The night's as bright as day and as quiet as the grave."

Twice up and down the length of the long attic we followed that elusive sibilance which kept what seemed about a yard ahead of us; and then abruptly the air in the attic was as silent as the frosty night without. The sound had apparently passed away through the blind gable-end.

"What can it have been?" I asked when we were back in the library.

"I reckon it were a ghost."

"You think it was?"

"I'm sure on it. It gave me the same feeling I had when I was walking up the garden one night and a ghost put his hand on my shoulder and let out a great puff right in my ear-hole."

"Did you see that ghost?" I asked incredulously.

"No, but we didn't see this one, come to that," my gardener retorted.

When that sound like the lisp of the wind in withered reeds ceased Search and I went downstairs and out into the garden. It was certainly not the wind. The night was so still that the flame of a lighted candle did not even faintly flicker. This happened fifty-six years ago as I write these words. From time to time I have returned to the occurrence in fancy and tried to suggest an explanation, but no explanation has ever presented itself.

Eighteen months later both Twinkle and Smut left this world. Twinkle was probably caught in some infernal gin and shot by a blasted keeper. Smut died of a uterine malady, only a little more than eight years old. She was a reddish-brown dog with a smut mask, and was never able to have puppies. I wrote a poem about her death which my sister Fay read recently in a broadcast. Several listeners wrote to ask me where they could find the poem, but the volume in which it appeared was published in 1907 and is very scarce to-day. So I reprint it in this book devoted to cats in order to show that I am not a dog-hater:

ELEGY ON THE DEATH OF A FAVOURITE BULLDOG

Thou need'st not any longer fear the snow,
And howl despondent when the driving rain
Bids thee frequent the rug and fireside-glow,
Or draws thee hopeless to the window pane:
For thee all winters have long gone before,
And endless Springs await thee evermore.

For now across an amaranthine field
The spirits of bad rabbits flee thy bark,

And haply some dread fox, sent unannealed
Below, is chased into the outer dark,
Where spectral traps and ghostly gins abound,
And through the gloom the hostile horns resound.

May no tall keeper's ghost thy steps affright,
May no malicious cat pursue thee dead,
And may no errand-boy's uneasy sprite
Fling vapour-woven baskets at thy head,
May all Plutonian dogs thy advent hail
And Cerberus in welcome wag his tail!

Sleep on in quiet meads of asphodel,
And if in dreams thy thoughts fly back to earth,
Dream kindly of us, faithful sentinel,
Who mourn the empty mat upon the hearth,
The idle collar and neglected plate,
Which on thy unfamiliar absence wait.

And when we shiver by the Stygian mere,
Above the lamentations through the dark,
Upon the bank remote, shall we not hear
A hollow and attenuated bark?
Then with the hero-dogs we'll see thee stand
Alert to greet us on the murky strand.

I still possess one relic of Smut in the shape of a chewed up volume of Malory's
Morte d'Arthur, an achievement of hers when she was a puppy in 1898.

Tootoose

I SHALL mention only one of the cats who lived with us when we went from Oxfordshire to Cornwall, and that was Tootoose. She was just an ordinary tabby, but she has a special place in my memory because she was my constant companion when I was writing my second novel *Carnival*. She used to wander around during the earlier part of the night and later climb up the magnolia tree against the side of the house and tap on the window of my study to be let in. Then she used to sit beside me on the writing-table at which in those days I still used to sit at work. Occasionally she would put a paw on my left hand to suggest that the sentence I was writing could wait a moment while I caressed her. She was with me on the night I finished the book and it was to her I confided that I thought, that indeed I was sure I had written the success of the year. *Carnival* has never been out of print except for a year or two at the beginning of the last war, and my hopes for its future were first confided to Tootoose about three o'clock of a December morning in 1911.

Tootoose had some delightful kittens of whom I remember best Derry and Toms.

" No goal ! "

" I didn't ask mother to get up here."

Pauline

IN 1914 Count Fersen, a wealthy and eccentric young Frenchman whose portrait I drew as Count Marsac in my novel *Vestal Fire*, brought to Capri from the Far East two Siamese kittens from the Royal household. The male kitten died on the voyage, and when the female grew up to be a queen, disregarding her rank, she had a love affair with a feline Lothario of humble stock. Two kittens were the result of this *mésalliance*, and before they were a month old their mother died. Fersen, who found that the mewling of the two kittens spoilt his opium dreams, asked my wife and me if we would take on the responsibility of bringing up the two diminutive creatures, and this we did. In that February of 1915 I had just begun to write *Guy and Pauline* and when the two babies arrived at Casa Solitaria we called the boy Guy and the girl Pauline. Guy was tortoiseshell with very little white: Pauline was tortoiseshell with equal markings of black and white.

They lived in the big studio which covered a third of the flat, the rest of it being a large tiled terrace surrounded by a parapet. I started work every afternoon about dusk and with a break for dinner used to sit, often until two or three in the morning, at the long table covered with green baize which Maxim Gorki had sold when after the outbreak of war he left Capri. From time to time I would get up to enjoy games with Guy and Pauline. I devised an elaborate series of tunnels out of newspapers in the maze of which Guy and Pauline would be set the problem of trying to discover one another. A basket was suspended from the ceiling in which the kittens were delighted to swing together and from which they were equally delighted to be able to eject one another, each of them king of the dizzy castle in turn.

Owing to their premature weaning the two of them used to suck each other's fur to the accompaniment of loud purrs and kneading paws. This habit had to be discouraged later, but Pauline would chew wool when she could for a long time afterwards and once chewed a large piece out of a friend's petticoat, having climbed up on her lap under her skirt.

Usually my wife and I walked along the Via Tragara to the Piazza before lunch and when the two kittens heard our voices along the path that led to the studio by a bridge over the gap that separated the rest of the house from the cliff they used to come bounding out to greet us. One day Pauline, in order to reach us before Guy, tried to jump over the gap at the back of the house and failing to reach the cliffside fell some twenty feet on to the cement below. When I reached her she was unhurt, but the sight of that wee creature disappearing from our view is still an agitating memory.

Soon after I left Capri for the Dardanelles my wife went back to England, when Guy and Pauline were looked after by a bachelor friend of ours. Presently he wrote to announce that Guy was a girl and suggested giving her away to somebody who wanted a kitten: he felt that Pauline by herself would be sufficient responsibility for a bachelor.

I saw Pauline again when I came back from Athens for a week's leave in November 1915 and after that I did not see her until I returned to Capri all but two years later. By then she had a marmalade husband called Pinkie. He had been the most successful of her lovers and had had to fight hard for her favours. She used to invite him in at first to have supper with her, and finally he was allowed to stay on the strict understanding that he was not to go wandering off at night after other cats.

When Pauline was staying at the Villa Cercola with our bachelor friend she used to sit on the pergola in his garden, the cynosure of a dozen or more Toms and when she came back to Casa Solitaria she missed this nightly tribute to her beauty.

So Pinkie was invited to live at Casa Solitaria and as she could not indulge in the admiration of a dozen males he was not allowed to indulge himself with the opposite sex.

Pinkie was kept severely in order by his wife. He was not allowed to begin to eat his lunch or his supper until she had tried both plates to see which tasted better. Then blinking nervously he would start.   If Pauline came across a morsel below her standard she would box Pinkie's ears, and he would at once stop eating to let her try his dish again.

After I got back to Capri at the end of 1917 she always slept in my bed unless she had unweaned kittens to look after. The preliminaries for the night never varied. While I was undressing she would walk round the plaster cornice, which was a Blondin feat. Then when I got into bed she would make a long and meticulous toilet while I read. This took at least a quarter of an hour; when it was finished she would jump up on the bed and snuggle down beside me with her head on my arm. I would be lying on my back with the book held up in front of me. Usually I would read for a least a couple of hours. She would lie perfectly still but sometimes when I turned over a page the slight movement of my arms would set her off purring.

When I had finished reading I would turn over on my left side and blow out the reading candle. Pauline would then turn over on her right side and sleep with her back stretched against my back and her head on the pillow.

Pauline much disliked being left at home when we went out. I recall an afternoon in March when the peach-trees were in full rosy bloom and the cliffside was splashed with wine-red anemones. Pauline accompanied us along the cliff path 400 feet above the silver-blue Salernian Gulf as far as the steps that led up to the Via Tragara.

"No Pauline, you can't come to tea with Mrs. Ross. You must go back home. You really must."

Pauline gave that low deep Siamese response which must be called a miaow, but which is a much superior noise to any ordinary miaow, that is unless it is delivered with an accelerating fortissimo, when it can be exasperating. With her colouring and great green eyes she was her father's daughter but her temperament and voice and chiffon-velvet fur were inherited from her royal mother.

"I don't want to go home," Pauline protested. "Pinkie is looking after the children, and I want to come out to tea with you."

She ran up the steps in front of us and jumped on to a low grey wall that ran along one side where the Via Tragara began.

"No, Pauline, you must go back. We may meet a big dog."

"Well, I'll walk along the top of this wall and no dog can touch me."

"No, Pauline, you are *not* coming out to tea. Go back home."

She watched us walking on along the Via Tragara, until we disappeared round the corner.

Presently we reached the steps going up to our hostess's tiny villa and were soon sitting at tea in her *salotto* which opened directly off the terrace. Five minutes later there came a tap on the door. Our hostess got up to admit the visitor, and Pauline entered the room. She boxed the ears of two Belgian griffon dogs who fled howling. Then she looked round her. An old lady guest was about to lift a thin slice of bread and butter to her mouth. Pauline jumped up on her lap and with her paw knocked the piece of bread and butter out of the old lady's hand on to the floor. She followed it and taking it to the choicest rug she could find she proceeded to eat the slice with a cat's deliberation. I never saw a tea-party quite so taken aback.

I told this story in a broadcast I gave well over thirty years ago and one listener wrote to express disapproval of such conduct in a cat. I suggested in my reply that at least he would credit a cat capable of behaving like this after walking a mile and a half away from her own home with profound confidence in the power of her own personality.

And that confidence Pauline certainly did have. She might walk along on top of a wall to avoid meeting dogs face to face but if she did meet them she yielded not an inch. I always pressed upon friends intending to call at Casa Solitaria not to bring their dogs with them. One day Dr. Axel Munthe arrived with his Aberdeen terrier. I advised him to leave the dog outside because Pauline disapproved of visiting dogs. He waved aside my warning. "Scottie (or some such name) can always look after himself," Munthe insisted.

The result was that Scottie went back to Anacapri that afternoon, leaving a bit of his nose behind him.

After she had brought up two or three families of kittens indoors Pauline decided that these children of hers received too much attention and carried away one by one the next family to a tiny cave about a hundred feet up the Telegrafo, the hill a thousand feet high from the sea which rose behind our house. Presumably her plan was that when they were weaned she would train them to look after themselves and not be spoilt by too much attention from human beings.

There was a carob tree overhanging the cliff path above which Pauline had her tiny den in the limestone, and it was her custom to spend some of her leisure time from domestic duties sitting on a branch of the carob. From this vantage point she would watch for the appearance of one of those lean rangy hounds which used to accompany the Capri *cacciatori* in their sporting onslaughts on the small birds of the island and retrieve the dead goldfinch or rock-thrush. Then as the hound came lolloping along the path Pauline would spring from her branch and land on its neck. The hound would rush on, howling, and when Pauline thought it had been sufficiently frightened she would take her claws out of its neck, jump off and go back to make sure that her kittens had not been molested.

We let Pauline indulge her fad for a week or two and then I told her firmly that the kittens must return to Casa Solitaria.

"You'll jump on a hound's neck once too often," I warned her. "And surely you can put up with your children about the place until we have found suitable homes for them."

Being a reasonable cat she accepted my ruling and when the kittens were brought back made no more attempts to move them.

To reward her display of common sense I gratified a desire she had long expressed. In the *salone* hung a large Venetian mirror among the rococo foliage of whose frame Pauline longed to climb but could not reach. She used to sit in the middle of the room, gazing earnestly at the mirror and from time to time uttering a deep miaow of thwarted ambition.

So I took her in my arms to the top of a step-ladder and lifted her on to the frame. She then climbed all round it, sniffing each individual gilded leaf until she could return from her exploration, satisfied that the frames of Venetian mirrors lacked interest for cats.

It was now her turn to give me a lesson. We were having a lunch-party to which one or two distinguished Capri visitors had been invited. When all was ready Carolina, our much beloved old maid, came in to announce "*È servito*" and I led the way into the dining-room to see Pauline, followed by four excited kittens, dragging a large crayfish by the tail backwards out of the dining room into the vestibule while the kittens were trying to seize its long antennae. The crayfish was as large as Pauline herself, but she found it fairly easy to move it over the porcelain tiling of the floor.

"Well," said Pauline when I rebuked her behaviour, "if you insist on keeping my kittens here you must expect me to provide for them."

Peter Scott, then about seven or eight years old, made a great impression on Pauline by producing three blue Faraglioni lizards out of his pocket. She herself was rarely able to catch one of the common green lizards and she felt that a boy who could capture three blue lizards would go far. And how right she was!

Pauline's end was a sad mystery. She went to stay with our old friend at the Villa Cercola when we left Casa Solitaria; one night she vanished and was never seen again. The general opinion was that she, like many other Capri cats had been caught, killed and eaten by some of the Milanese workmen who had been imported to the island to begin the process of transforming it from the enchanted island of Capri into the vulgar isle of Capree.

Pauline was my constant companion during the writing of *Guy and Pauline*, *Sylvia Scarlet*, *Poor Relations*, *Rich Relatives* and *The Vanity Girl*. She is with me now in memory—cradled in my arms and purring gently as I read, lying back to back with me in bed, her head upon the pillow, or sleeping before a fire of chestnut logs through a long wintry night of work. *Soror, ave atque vale.*

Bing

THE first authority on Siamese cats I ever knew was the late Sir Stephen Gazelee, and the tales of Gazelee's two cats at Magdalene College, Cambridge nearly sixty years ago now, rivalled the exploits of the Nemean lion. In October 1916 Ronald Storrs and I went up to Cambridge for a wonderful weekend with Gazelee, Storrs leaving on Monday morning to go and govern Jerusalem and myself returning to a crisis in Athens. Gazelee's famous cats were dead by then, but he had had their skins dressed and could still stroke what was left of his old friends' fur draped over each arm of his favourite chair.

A few weeks later I was on Syra in the middle of the Cyclades and to my delight was presented with a Siamese kitten by friends on the island. In moments of the most acute exacerbation when we in Syra were having to handle careerist generals or consuls suffering from aggravated consulitis Bing, as that kitten was called, could always calm us to a smile by his superb clowning. We used to watch him for an hour at a time after dinner fighting with a long feather duster, a sport of which neither he nor we tired. Every morning Bing drove in the car from the old Turkish consulate where some of us lived to the office of the Aegean Intelligence Service. Here he was loved by everybody but perhaps most of all by the porters on guard in the courtyard.

In that month of June 1917 the heat was terrific and it was not allayed by the foulness of the bread, which was now apparently made of mud and straw. Still, we had our light moments, one of which was provided by a Greek torpedo-boat that was moored stern on to the quay opposite the windows of our office. One of my subalterns had just come back from a mission on which I had sent him to one of the islands and was seated in the small room wherein officers return-

23

ing from a job were at once set down to write their reports before they had time to indulge in embroidering their experiences.

Suddenly there was a shattering roar, and when I rushed out from my room to find out what had happened I saw young Macartney standing in the passage with a bewildered expression on his chubby face and heard the occupants in the large central office beyond buzzing like disturbed bees.

"It went right through the wall underneath my chair," young Macartney quavered, his face with emotion growing younger and younger all the time until it looked like that of a four-year-old child who had been pushed over by a companion.

"Went through underneath your chair? What went through underneath your chair?"

"A shell," said Macartney. "I was writing my report."

"You certainly were," I laughed.

"No, really, this shell did go through under my chair. You can see the hole under the table. That's where it came through and buried itself in the wall without bursting."

And sure enough Macartney was speaking the simple truth. The after gun of the Greek torpedo-boat, which was pointed directly at our office hardly ten yards away, had been left loaded, and presently the terrific heat of the weather had caused the shell to leave the gun. If the shell had exploded it would have been the end of Macartney and probably quite a few other people. As it was, how we laughed!

Then suddenly we all became serious on hearing that Bing had vanished, and when he was nowhere to be found we were beginning to wonder if by some horrible mischance that beloved little creature had been in the path of the shell. We had been searching for him in every cranny of the offices and in the courtyard at the back when we heard at the window of the house next door loud screams from a woman who was shrieking that her bedridden mother had been attacked by the Devil.

To our immense relief the Devil turned out to be Bing who, frightened by the explosion, had rushed up the chimney in the main office whence he had found his way down another chimney into the bedroom of the old lady next door. Now, covered with soot he was standing with arched back, spitting at her from the foot of the bed.

" It's not a real bird at all."

" Mother can't lie like this, she'd fall off."

" *I* didn't drink th[
milk."

Three months later I had to part with Bing when I left Syra. It would have been impossible to take him with me on the long wartime journey to London and I had no idea where or what my next job was likely to be. So I gave him to some Syra friends and he lived as happily as a grown-up cat as he had lived through his kittenhood.

Sylvia the First

In the autumn of 1920 I succeeded in securing from the Crown a sixty-year lease of the Channel Islands of Herm and Jethou, and a couple of months after I took up residence early in the following year I acquired a Siamese kitten whom I called Sylvia after the heroine of my novel *Sylvia Scarlett*.

From the first that small Siamese kitten was entirely devoted to me and I loved her just a little more than I have loved any cat. She had a stumpy tail with an unusually pronounced double kink which even as long ago as that would have been regarded with horror by any member of the Siamese Cat fancy. To-day a tiny kink at the very tip of the tail is frowned upon, although it does not actually disqualify the cat who has it from gaining an award when shown.

Let me take this opportunity of saying that I regard the attempt to weed out the kink as a deplorable example of the rage for standardization which already handicaps and may in time arrest the mental development of democracy. The kink of the Siamese tail and the squint in the Siamese eyes do not deserve to be eliminated. There is a pleasant tale about the origin of the kink. A Siamese princess of long ago used to take her favourite cat with her when she bathed in a secluded pool in the royal gardens, and it was her habit before going into the water to remove her rings and slip them over her cat's tail. Then one day in the excitement of seeing a goldfish in the pool the cat swished its tail and as it did so the rings were swished into the pool. To prevent such an accident recurring in the future the princess bent her cat's tail into a kink at the tip so that if it was swished again at the sight of goldfish the rings would stay safely where she had put them.

In those first two or three months on Herm I was much alone and working late at night to finish a novel called *The Seven Ages of Woman* in order to begin the

26

formidable task of writing a trilogy about the life of a Church of England parson. After dinner every night I settled down in the invalid chair in which I have had to write since 1913 to fend off the attacks of an acute sciatica. In this chair after my man had brought in a pint of ale at eleven o'clock Sylvia used to lie beside me without moving until I went off to bed about four or five, when she accompanied me upstairs and got into bed with me. Until Thompson came in last thing at night with the pint of ale it was her habit to use my black Great Dane as a couch. Hamlet was expected to lie outstretched in front of the fire until the time came for him to go off to his kennel with Thompson at eleven o'clock. Siamese cats always enjoy lying with their front paws slightly higher than their backsides. Sylvia found that the stomach of a Great Dane provided her with the perfect medium for this attitude. Hamlet was not expected to move. A disapproving low growl from Sylvia warned him to keep still.

Hamlet: (*with propitiatory thumps of his tail*). Do you mind if I get up for a moment, turn round and lie down again on my other side?

Sylvia: (*growling*). Why do you want to be so fidgety? You'll be going off to your kennel in another hour.

Hamlet: Yes, but I'm getting pins and needles.

Sylvia: (*growling again*). Pins and needles, my paws! Do you expect me to get out of the comfortable position I'm in merely because you have a fancy to lie on your left side instead of your right side? Just like a dog! Always must fidget.

Hamlet with a deep sigh that was very near to a groan would give up the argument and remain on his right side until Thompson arrived with my nightcap of ale and he was no longer compelled to be an immobile couch for that Siamese kitten.

"Mew!" Sylvia would exclaim as she settled herself down beside me in the chair. "Queer awkward creatures dogs, aren't they? But I must admit that as dogs go Hamlet is not too bad. He's gawky and fidgety and extremely stupid, but he's not a bad old sort."

Sylvia herself had always taken her exercise before we reached the room where I was working. She had her dinner in the kitchen while I was having my soup and always arrived in the dining-room when the parlour-maid brought in the fish or entrée. Then she would jump on the mahogany table and sit for the rest of the meal on a mat which was placed at my left-hand to spare her the discomfort of the bare board. She never moved from her mat until a dish of filberts appeared with dessert. Then a paw was placed on my hand to remind me that it was time for the evening game. As I stripped the nut she would watch me, all tensed for the great moment when I would send the nut rolling down the table to the floor. After a game of football all over the floor of the room she would jump back on the table with the nut in her mouth and again I would send it rolling over the table for another game of football. At last she would tire of the exercise and leaving the nut in a corner she would jump back on the table and tell me that it was time to quit the dining-room and adjourn to the fire in my workroom where Hamlet was expected to remain outstretched on the hearthrug for her to turn him into a couch.

Another game she enjoyed was lying on the palms of my hands to be tossed up to the ceiling and caught. She would keep herself stiff all the way up and come down equally stiff on to my hands. She also enjoyed lying on her back and being given a somersault to land on her feet.

I thought it would be good for Sylvia to have a companion of her own age and that spring I bought a blue Persian kitten. She was called Lily after the indolent and beautiful girl who lived with Sylvia Scarlett. As in the book Sylvia Scarlett dominated Lily Haden so Sylvia the kitten dominated Lily the kitten from the start, and that without so much as one angry spit.

One of the obligations in my lease of Herm was to allow the public access to the famous shell beach three times a week on payment of a sixpenny toll of which fourpence was retained by me and twopence by King George V as Duke of Normandy. During that glorious summer of 1921 those visitors were the only cloud upon its azure serenity. Access to the shell beach gave them about a hundred acres of pasturage and a mile of coast to defile with their litter but that toll of sixpence convinced them that they were entitled to wander all over the island. Quiet inoffensive people at home were turned into aggressive savages by the tricky three miles of sea between Guernsey and Herm. Robinson Crusoe did not observe the arrival of a war-canoe on his island with more apprehension than I would watch those visitors disembark in our little harbour.

I must have communicated my feelings to Sylvia. On the three tripper days she was always to be seen in a window of the White House where I was still living while the ugly pseudo-Gothic house at the top of the island occupied by my predecessor Prince Blücher was being made habitable. Later on I opened the Mermaid Tavern for such visitors in the White House, a name which I believe it still retains. As they landed and walked along the quay Sylvia would growl at them until they had disappeared along the road leading to the Shell Beach. However, if those visitors could ignore the signpost and take the other direction they would constantly do so. On one occasion Sylvia, her stumpy tail bristling, came into the drawing room where a friend and I were having our coffee after lunch to announce in contralto Siamese that two of the savages had dared to walk into the White House.

And sure enough a couple of our visitors followed that indignant kitten into the room. When I suggested that this part of the island was private one of them observed with what he evidently hoped was crushing sarcasm,

"I thought we lived in a free country."

There is a Siamese vocal outburst to which "Wow!" is the nearest I can get on the page.

"Wow!" exclaimed Sylvia.

No argument about the degree of freedom enjoyed by Britons ensued because at that moment Hamlet arrived in the room carrying a pair of lacy panties in his mouth.

"My dog evidently thinks so too," I said.

Hamlet had not deprived some bather on the shell beach of her panties. He had found them on a small beach on the far side of the island to bathe from which was not included in the privileges allowed to our invaders for their sixpenny toll, and whatever young woman went back to Guernsey that evening without her panties was silent about their loss.

That cloudless summer of 1921 lingered on well into October, and work on the first volume of my trilogy was sadly behind time when I returned to it that winter and was much interrupted by pain. *The Altar Steps* was a very difficult book to write and without the constant presence of that little cat beside me in my chair I believe I should have abandoned the task of finishing it in time for publication in 1922.

In March it was settled that Sylvia's marriage must be arranged. There was no eligible young Siamese Tom in Guernsey, and I decided to buy one from a breeder in England whose advertisement I had seen in some paper. I was not a member of the Siamese Cat Club at this date; indeed, I was unaware of its existence. Therefore when answering the advertisement of Siamese kittens for sale I did not enquire into the reputation of the breeder.

In due course the husband arrived whose marriage had been arranged with Sylvia in the future. She took one look at him, spat, hurried up to my bedroom, got into bed, went down to the foot of it and bit my toe.

By evening the yellowish froth of gastro-enteritis was round the mouth of the new arrival and within twenty-four hours he was dead. These were the days before inoculation, and few were the Siamese cats that recovered from an attack. It is a highly infectious disease, and for a breeder to send away a kitten which had been exposed to infection in a cattery was disgraceful. Some years later this breeder was censured by the Siamese Cat Club for some breach of cattery etiquette and resigned from it. He then tried to start a rival club, but his malicious enterprise was stillborn.

I have always felt that when Sylvia bit my toe that morning she was trying to warn me of the threat the new arrival was to herself. She had welcomed Lily, and some months ago she had welcomed a Sealyham called Stella to whom she had persistently tried to impart some of her own intelligence. Indeed, the only big creatures she disliked were trippers in a herd.

That new arrival was her death-warrant. A day or two later the menacing yellow froth was oozing from her lips. She was not left alone for a minute during the next forty-eight hours but nothing we could do was able to save that little life. Just before she died she twitched her stumpy tail twice as I leaned over her. It was her last effort to show me she recognized I was doing all I could.

I have never been so much affected by the loss of an animal and as I write about her now nearly forty years later, sitting in the same chair where once upon a time she kept me company through the night as I struggled with *The Altar Steps*, I still miss her, and I have never forgiven that feline breeder who betrayed the code of the Siamese Cat Club.

At the time I could not bear to remain in the White House and although the cottage joined to the Manor House in which I intended to live was not yet ready I moved into it the day after Sylvia died. But I never really recovered on Herm from the loss of Sylvia. I began to feel that the island was unlucky to me, and soon after this I was told something which confirmed this feeling.

My predecessor Prince Blücher von Wahlstatt had been a victim of the hysteria that seizes a country with the outbreak of war and in 1914 he had not been allowed to return, the usual nonsensical fantasies about gun-emplacements and the rest of it being rife. He had married a younger Princess Radziwill whose elder sister married his son at the same time. By this double marriage Prince Blücher became the father-in-law of his sister-in-law and Count Lothair Blücher the son-in-law of his sister-in-law. Count Lothair and Countess Blücher were still living on Guernsey, the Count having been accorded what was held to be the privilege of a commission in a labour battalion but not allowed to serve with the forces in the field during the war. Soon after Sylvia's death I was dining with the Blüchers and the Countess told me that when the news came that Prince and Princess Blücher were not to be allowed to return to the island they loved so much the Princess had wished ill-fortune to the next tenant of the island.

"But she did not know it would be somebody like you or she would never have done what she did."

So far as I was concerned Herm was ill-wished, to use a Cornish phrase, and putting aside any mysterious malign influence I found the financial burden of running the island too much for my pen. One day I appealed to the elemental spirits of the island to send a war profiteer to relieve me of it. Two hours later they sent across in his yacht Sir Percival Perry who had bought the " Slough Dump" and in the following year I was able to transfer to him the lease of Herm and retire myself to the very much smaller island of Jethou. When Sylvia died I gave Lily away because her presence was too poignant a reminder of another's absence. So there was no cat on Jethou when Sylvia the Second arrived as a small kitten.

Sylvia the Second and Michael

IT may seem strange that I should have called another kitten Sylvia but from
the moment she arrived I recognized that she was worthy to bear the name of
that beloved first Sylvia. At the same time I resolved not to seek to make her
dependent on my company nor to make myself dependent upon hers.

Sylvia the Second was a granddaughter of Champion Bonzo, and in the evolu-
tion of the typical Siamese cat of to-day Champion Bonzo enjoys a renown equal
to that of Eclipse in the story of the thoroughbred race horse. I doubt if any
champion of to-day is without a drop of Champion Bonzo's blood on its paternal
or maternal side. There are, apart from *the* Siamese Cat Club, Siamese Cat Clubs
in France, Belgium, the United States and South Africa, and probably elsewhere
in the world. Descendants of Champion Bonzo will be found in all of them.
I had the privilege of shaking paws with him once over thirty years ago and I
pay this brief tribute to the memory of a really great cat.

Sylvia was from the start a dominating and completely integrated personality.
She was what the Italians call *prepotente* without ever being tiresomely self-
assertive. She seldom miaowed—except when in love. Then she was capable of
contralto vocalism that would almost have silenced Dame Clara Butt. She had
enough commonsense to know that on the little island of Jethou no lover lurked,
and she may have tried to make herself heard on Herm in the hope of luring some
feline Leander across the Hellespont that separated the two islands.

Jethou is a very small island, scarcely a mile round and fifty acres in extent.
It rises from the sea in the shape of a steep tumulus to the height of 262 feet,
and is guarded north and south by two small Mont Saint Michels, known as
Creviçon (the prawny place) and La Grande Fauconnaire (the great falconry).
In the small space it occupies Jethou provides a variety of scene which no island

32

" There's that cat from next door in our garden again."

" We had a kitten like that at our school."

of similar size anywhere round the coasts of Great Britain, Ireland or France can offer. Moreover, it has a grove of ancient Spanish chestnuts, pears and hawthorns and in the walled garden by the cliff's edge there is an umbrageous mulberry-tree nearly 250 years old.

At the low spring tides a large tract of sand was exposed round Creviçon, the rocky pools about which were full of large prawns. Those who have lived with Siamese cats know that they regard prawns as a tip-top delicacy. Indeed there was only one dish that Sylvia preferred and that was pâté de foie gras. I never tried her with caviare, but if she had known that it was even more expensive than pâté de foie gras no doubt she would have preferred caviare.

However, the outstanding attraction of Jethou for cats was the plenitude of rabbits. An Elizabethan Governor of Guernsey introduced them and over three centuries ago Drayton in his *Polyolbion* wrote of Jethour and its conies. Siamese cats prefer rabbit as a staple diet to anything else. Only very occasionally did any of my cats on Jethou bother about catching birds. Rabbits were what they enjoyed hunting, not to play with them as birds and mice are played with by cats but to kill and eat them at once, leaving behind nothing but the gizzard and the scut.

After the tragic result of arranging a future husband for Sylvia the First I postponed as long as I could the arrival of a husband for Sylvia the Second. Such an event for our own peace could not be postponed indefinitely, and in due course Michael came to us from a conscientious breeder whose cattery was free of that foul gastro-enteritis.

Michael's parents had been native Siamese. His coat was a rich tawny, his points chocolate. His mask was not V-shaped like a marten's but rounded. His tail had a decided kink at the tip and his eyes were like sapphires. By this date Michael was out of fashion, so rapid had been the development of the Westernized type we accept as the standard to-day for Siamese cats.

Michael and Sylvia became friends immediately. Naturally it was to be expected that Michael would be friends with her, but it was surprising that she made up her mind about him so quickly. It might fairly have been called love at first sight. Indeed, we all loved Michael, who was the sweetest cat imaginable with a gentle little mew to express his affection, for not even that gentle little mew was ever used to express anything except affection.

When he became the father of four children, two males and two females, he

5

used to visit his wife and family, sniff and lick the kittens first and then kiss Sylvia before he left them, always to be back again in not more than an hour to do the same thing all over again.

In due course I gave away the two female kittens but kept Stumps and Baron, the two male kittens. Stumps, who was Sylvia's firstborn, had a short tail with a double kink like the tail of my beloved first Sylvia. Apart from his tail he took after his mother both in disposition and appearance. He had her complete self-assurance but being a male he was inclined to show off with it. He lacked the confident and unperturbed serenity of his mother's bearing. A visit with Baron, his brother, to the vet in Guernsey, did not shake that self-assurance. When he returned and his mother asked him what he thought he was now he boxed her ears. It was the only time I ever saw Sylvia for a moment completely taken aback.

Baron except for being of a much lighter colour took after his father and had the same gentle mew. He was not so active as Stumps and concentrated in his hunting on baby rabbits. As the rabbits on Jethou were a plague and I objected to trapping them I was grateful to Baron, who during the seven years he spent on the island must have killed and eaten not less than 4,000 baby rabbits. Death was always instantaneous and only when prawns were about did Baron show a lively interest in the domestic meal.

Of the endless games I played with kittens the one that gave me most amusement was a game I invented with the envelopes of ten-inch gramophone records. To play this a kitten must be old enough for the hole in the middle of the envelope not to slip off when its neck is encircled. When the kittens saw one another looking like the horses of knights at a tournament they would start tilting at one another, advancing and retreating sideways in the most ludicrous attitudes of defiance.

And then this family life was suddenly broken up by Michael. It was as I remember just after his second mating with Sylvia that one morning I heard what sounded like demoniac yells coming from the garden. I rushed out to see Stumps at one end of a bough in the mulberry-tree along which Michael with a ferocious squint, every hair of his coat standing up, was stalking his eldest son. The Hanoverian Georges would have applauded such treatment of an heir; we deplored it.

I half expected Michael to turn on me when I pulled him down from the mulberry-tree, but he at once returned to his gentle self. The next day he was again in pursuit of Stumps and his intention undoubtedly was to kill him if possible.

Baron decided that his life was in danger too and retired to the other side of the island.

I did not want to lose either him or Stumps but I did not want to lose Michael either, and I felt that the only thing to do was to send him over to the vet in Guernsey and deny him any more opportunities of becoming a patriarch.

It was no good. He was just as fierce as ever with his sons, and foreseeing that his next sons by Sylvia would be as much the object of his vengeance in a few month's time as Stumps and Baron I sought a home for him elsewhere. So he retired to a country house near Dumfries and lived happily with people who loved him. He enjoyed hunting and was shot at last by some wretched keeper.

The departure of Michael meant that Sylvia would have to find a husband overseas. She was not in the least upset by the Channel crossing and never made any fuss about being put into her travelling basket when the time came for a honeymoon. She was, as I said, a cat endowed with remarkable commonsense.

One day she decided that the trouble of scratching in her tray when she merely wished to perform number one could be obviated by following the example of human beings and using the seat provided for them. She could not pull the plug, but I have no doubt that if it had been possible she would have done so. I have not heard of any other cat that was accustomed to use a w.c. like this and I regret that we never managed to get a snapshot of her performance which was a perfectly judged balancing feat. Whether she tried to teach any of her children to emulate her I do not know, but if she did she was unsuccessful. If anybody who reads this has known of a cat that did what Sylvia did I should be glad to hear of it. I have never heard of such a performance by any other cat.

Sylvia was a model mother and all her kittens were as strictly brought up as the human children of once upon a time. She nursed them with devoted regularity until she decided it was time to wean them. Then a moment would come when the kittens came joyfully to greet her in expectation of a meal, only to be received with menacing growls, spits, and cuffs. Poor little things, they would stare at one another, asking what had happened to the old girl. Then one of them would be egged on by his brothers and sisters to try again. He was soon retreating from his mother's growls, ears twitching from the cuff he had been given. However, as soon as her children realized that there was an end to suckling she would encourage them to cuddle into her. This would last for about a month and then abruptly she would let them know that they were too big now to be sprawling about all over her. Then came a day when Sylvia decided that there were too many cats about the house and some time before they were to be weaned she lured her latest litter to a wall at the top of the island in which there was a cosy cavelet.

She and I had an argument about the future when we discovered at last where Sylvia had hidden her kittens.

Self. Look here, Sylvia, you can't expect your kittens to be able to hunt rabbits for themselves before they are at least three months old and even then they will have to rely entirely on baby rabbits.

Sylvia. So what?

Self. They must come back to the house. They'll find out where the house is when you leave them to fend for themselves, and I do *not* want to see you behaving in the way dear Michael behaved to his sons.

Sylvia. They're my kittens.

Self. Yes, I agree they *are* your kittens, and you must face up to maternal responsibility.

Sylvia. I *am* facing up to it.

Self. Suppose they starve?

Sylvia. That will be their look-out. I shall teach them how to catch rabbits.

Self. Sylvia, please don't be so obstinate. You know what a shock it is to your kittens when you decide that the moment has come for weaning them. It's quite a different matter teaching kittens how to eat porridge out of a saucer from teaching them how to catch rabbits. Anyway, I can't spend any more time arguing with you in this wind. You're comfortable enough in your small cave but I'm being blown to pieces. The kittens are to come back to the house. I have brought up a basket for them, and I assume you don't intend to spend the night up here by yourself. Now, please, no growls. I know you have a will of your own, but so have I, and no amount of growling will prevent my taking the kittens back to the house.

Sylvia squinted at me intently for a minute or two. Then she emerged from the wall and accompanied me back to the house.

We used to give away the girls when they were six months old, but I became much attached to one of them called Venetia and I decided to keep her. Knowing that she and Sylvia could not hope to agree unless Venetia was freed from the fetters of love I sent Venetia into Guernsey to be spayed. In those days it was an unusual operation for a vet to perform and Venetia died from the effects of it. This greatly upset me and twenty-five years were to pass before I could bring myself to take the risk again.

At low spring tides when we all went prawning round Creviçon the cats used to sit in the glass veranda on the south side of the house and watch with concentrated anticipation the prawners at work. Then they would follow the catch to the kitchen, outside the door of which they would yowl in unison until one of our maids emerged with a dish full of pink prawns and brought it from the adjacent cottage where the kitchen was to the dining-room. All the cats would then come charging down the path beside whichever maid was coming with the prawns, who, as pink as the prawns she was carrying, would somehow put the dish on the table and shut the cats out until we sat down to tea. Then the cats were admitted and as fast as we pulled off the heads and the tails and threw them on the floor they were gobbled up. It was an indecorous scene of greedy ecstasy, but one to which I look back with a loving smile.

I have just been reading an enchanting story about a cat called *The Nine Lives of Island Mackenzie* which by the time these words are in print will be a year old as a book. If those who may read these reminiscences of mine have not read Miss Ursula Moray Williams' delightful tale they will be grateful for my recommendation of it. At one point Island Mackenzie is irritated by the attention paid to a parrot and as I sympathize with that adventurous cat I remember how much my own Sylvia used to resent a cockatoo brought to the island by a friend of ours. She used to ask me why this noisy white bird had to have his perch in her favourite veranda. I tried to explain to her what hospitality meant but she was not impressed.

"Why should I give up my favourite haunt because I cannot stand the screeching of that detestable bird?" she asked. "Those white gobblers you brought to the island were bad enough." She was referring to the importation of a white turkey-cock with two white turkey-hens who had made life intolerable for our cats by gobbling after them with arrogant self-consciousness. Fortunately for their peace of mind the turkey-cock took to attacking the human beings and was banished from the island after which the two wives were eaten, and of course the cats had their share.

Sylvia stuck to her cushion in the veranda as long as she could, and then one day I came in to find her growling at the cockatoo, obviously threatening to knock him off his perch if he did not stop his loathsome screeching. But that only made him screech louder. At last with a yowl of baffled rage and half a dozen vicious spits Sylvia's ears could stand it no longer and she fled from the veranda. Nor would she enter it again until the cockatoo had been removed to the bungalow where our carpenter and his wife were housed. Here he lived happily, growing greyer every year from the smoke of a stove that in certain winds gushed out in volumes in spite of experimenting with a series of different cowls on the chimney.

Stumps, Baron, Bimbo and Boy

I HAD great hopes of Bimbo, who was one of Michael's second family. He was a most amusing kitten. I had a small swing door cut in the door of my library so that the cats could come in and go out without my having to get up from my chair to open the door for them. I thought it was my own idea but discovered later that Cardinal Mazarin had anticipated me by some three hundred years. When he was three months old Bimbo used to arrive in the library every evening at exactly half-past six o'clock with a pellet of paper. This was carried to the far end of the room over forty feet long where I would be working in my chair. Then the pellet would be dropped on the floor and Bimbo would sit, waiting for me to pick it up and throw it to the other end of the library. After he had retrieved the paper half a dozen times he would then decide he had had enough and picking up his pellet would retire with it through the small swing door and put it in a safe place until half-past six the following evening. Alas, Bimbo did not bear out the promise of his youth as a character. He became obsessed by the notion of eating and though courteous and responsive to a caress one always had the feeling that the courtesy and the affection were displayed merely in the hope that one had something for him to eat. However, in spite of his preoccupation Bimbo lived until he was nearly nineteen years old. Perhaps it was the overwhelming personality of Stumps, Sylvia's first born, which prevented Bimbo's development and also that of Boy who was the offspring of one of Sylvia's later marriages. Boy was highly strung and everybody who has been associated with Siamese cats knows what that means. If they are nervous they are never cured of nerves. I think that is equally true of human beings in spite of the claims put forward by psychotherapy.

Against my better judgment I had given away a nervy female kitten who had panicked in her new home, and at the slightest excuse rushed off to hide in the chimney. In the end she had to be put to sleep. I made up my mind never again to give away such an animal and when Boy whom I had promised to another friend began to show signs of ' nerves ' I decided he must stay with the family, particularly as he was devoted to Nellie Boyte, one of my secretaries, and also, be it added, to the splendid rabbit hunting on Jethou.

To come back to Stumps. Except for that disqualifying short tail with a double kink he represented the Siamese neuter at its superlative best. I loved that tail of his because it reminded me of my beloved first Sylvia; in any case I have made it a rule never to exhibit or sell any of my cats. Stumps had a personality which matched his outward form. I always felt that he had taunted his father with having been reduced to the same status as himself and that this may have been the reason why Michael was still determined to kill his eldest son even after the operation that was intended to remove any cause for jealousy. From the moment Michael left us to go and live in Scotland Stumps assumed the chieftainship of Clan Chattan on Jethou. Not that he ventured to put on airs in front of his mother. Sylvia was a matriarch in the grand tradition who ruled her children from the moment they were born. There was, I have to admit, an embarrassing moment in my library when Stumps tried (most ineffectively) to play Œdipus to his mother. At the moment she was suffering from the pangs of unassuaged love and did not protest, but when she returned from her marriage on the mainland the first thing she did on getting out of her travelling basket was to clout her eldest son who never again ventured to take any liberties with her.

Stumps could never understand our inability to control the weather. If we could provide fires for him why were we unable to turn on the sun? If we could exclude draughts from a room why were we unable to calm the wind? He would stand on the steps and yowl indignantly in the open door.

"I want to go out and do my business in the garden. Good lord, do you think I'm going out in all that streaming wet? Turn it off. Can't turn it off? What do you mean, 'can't turn it off?' All right, I warn you if I have to scratch half the contents out of our box of sand it will be your own fault. And it may not stop there, I may decide to perform on somebody's bed."

There is a superstition that May cats are dirty cats. Sylvia's first litter came in May but under her severe bringing up they were all scrupulously clean, except Stumps. His occasional defiance of sanitation, however, was deliberate and intended to punish us for not turning off the rain or turning on the sun.

" I'll get it for you, mother.   You're not as quick as you were
when you were my age."

" I'll soon learn to dance on my toes without holding on to anything."

In order to punish him I had a trapdoor cut in the floor of my library down which he was banished to wander about in the dark under the floor until he had served his sentence. Even imprisonment he once turned to his own advantage, for when I raised the trapdoor he jumped back into the room with a rat in his mouth.

"Ha-ha! Sucks to you," he said. "Do you see how I've been amusing myself?" When I exclaimed in astonishment he twitched his tail cockily.

"Yes, I thought you'd be a bit surprised by the way I can amuse myself when you shut me up in that boring place underneath."

But my exclamation had not been prompted by surprise over Stumps' feat. My surprise was to find that he had killed an old English black rat, the only one I ever saw in my life. Our Jethou rats were brown monsters which lived by the sea-shore, eating limpets and sucking sea-birds' eggs. I believe that black rat was the last of his race, a sort of Harold defying the Norman invaders.

Baron was completely different in temperament from Stumps. He was a very large cat but less muscular than his elder brother, and he had for so large a cat that ridiculous squeak of a mew not at all like the contralto of his mother or the deep indignant yowl of which Stumps was capable when things did not at once go exactly the way he wished them to go. Yet in all their long lives of eighteen years I never saw Stumps and Baron quarrel. This may have been because Baron always deferred to Stumps in an argument; if that was so his deference was completely dignified. He got his name from his uniform light colouring. At the time of his birth mustard was being advertised through a character called the Baron de Beef. Baron as a kitten being the colour of mustard became the Baron de Beef. I have already mentioned Baron's prowess with baby rabbits, and he was such a gentle kindly creature that I always fancied him eating those young rabbits with the mournful sympathy of the walrus and the carpenter devouring the young oysters.

Over thirty years ago I ran into Lance Sieveking during a visit to London and he asked why I never broadcast. I told him I had been offered a weekly talk about gramophone records after one I had done in 1923 but that I had not felt it worth-while to make the journey from the Channel Isles.

"Well, you must do a talk. What would you like to talk about?" he asked.

"What about a talk on Siamese cats?"

"Siamese cats?" he murmured doubtfully. "Do you think people will be interested in them? I thought you might like to talk about your island."

6

"Well, what about 'Siamese Cats and Some Islands' as a title?" I suggested.

This was accepted and it was arranged for a date at the beginning of October. I opened as follows:

"I am feeling guilty at this moment, because I have always considered it unpardonable for anybody to talk about his pets, and I am only sustained by a conviction that the Siamese cat is just the pet that lots of people are wanting. I am not trying to gain the sympathy of prejudiced listeners when I say that it combines all that is best in cats and dogs, because I am not prepared as a fanatical lover of the cat to admit that the cat requires to borrow any virtues from the dog. Still, the personal devotion of the dog to its master is one of its glories, and even more attractive to my mind is the personal devotion of the Siamese cat not to its master, but in what I think is a finer relationship, to its friend. I accept all that their lovers may say about the dog and the horse. But the Siamese cat is just as capable of personal devotion, and it will sacrifice all that a cat holds most dear for the sake of that devotion. To illustrate this I cannot resist quoting from a letter which reached me yesterday, 'This beloved cat lived a most adventurous life with us in India for many years and went everywhere with us. I have carried him on my horse, he has ridden on a camel, camped out, lived on a houseboat in Kashmir, motored and trained thousands of miles . . . after the war I had to leave him with a friend in India. Returning after two years he knew me at once. We brought him home, and he only died this February, being fifteen years old.' . . . .

"The Siamese cat is indeed an animal of most definite likes and dislikes, and unless it likes you naturally no amount of coaxing or bribery on your part will ever win its affection. The origin of the Siamese cat is obscure, but the most satisfactory theory makes it an inbred, semi-albino variety of the Malay jungle cat, and no relation to any Western cat. The markings are rather like those of a Jersey cow, that is to say, its body is cream or *café au lait* or tawny with seal or chocolate points. The tail can be straight, but the more characteristic tail is kinked at the tip. The fur is fine and close, and silky as a chinchilla rabbit's, and when plenty of outdoor exercise is available to keep it in condition this fur is delicately perfumed like a sachet. The mask is V-shaped like a marten's, and the eyes are of a blue which sometimes exceeds in intensity that radiant blue in the heart of ice. Such an animal at first glance does not look like a cat at all. My friend and publisher, Newman Flower, once told me a story of somebody who lived in Vauxhall Bridge Road, and who kept about a dozen Siamese which he used to take out with him in the evening when he went to post his letters. On one occasion an astonished navvy passing by called out to a friend:

" 'Bill, look at this bloke walking about the blooming street with a lot of blinking otters.'

"And I have heard my own cats called monkeys before now."

I went on to tell some of the stories about Pauline and Bing on Capri and Syra and after a brief description of Jethou I wound up:

"I suppose I ought to mention some of the faults of Siamese cats before I stop. They are very jealous, and suffer acutely from it. They are—yes, it must be admitted—very greedy. They think that Samarkand rugs were only woven to be pulled to pieces by their own sharp claws. They have no idea of doing without something they want, and if they want anything they make a noise till they get it. But what are their faults compared with their virtues—with their sense of humour, their fidelity, their dauntless courage (unless they think they have seen a ghost when they will tear away like so many animated hearth brushes), their playfulness (it is up to you to provide the game, they will play it), their conversational powers (if you have Siamese cats you must talk to them a lot), their awareness of themselves (so that every one of my cats knows its own name and will respond to it with a twitch of the tail however many of them are lying about in the room), their love of people rather than place, their honesty (by which I mean they'll take a lobster off the table in front of you), their continuous passionate interest in all that is going on around them, and their depth of affection, which they are able to show in so many exquisite ways?"

At the end of my talk I had time to tell listeners that if they had been interested by what I had been saying about Siamese cats they might like to know that the annual show of the Siamese Cat Club was being held next week at St. Cuthbert's Parish Hall, Philbeach Gardens.

I went back to Jethou but a week later I received a letter from the late Phyl Wade, who was then the devoted secretary of the Siamese Cat Club, to say that the attendance at the Show had been ten times as large as it had ever been and that I had been unanimously elected as President of the Club. And I am still President, though alas, that most lovable woman Phyl Wade is no longer with us.

I never had more than six fully grown cats on Jethou at once, but there were always at least another half dozen half grown as well. These younger ones waiting for suitable homes were all given names and there was not one that did not answer to its name by the time it was two months old. I often went for a walk round the island, followed by about ten cats of various ages, not to mention a bobtail sheepdog and a couple of Sealyhams. None of the cats or dogs was gun-shy and all applauded the end of one of those pestilential rabbits. I did enjoy shooting rabbits, and it had to be done for the sake of our flowers and shrubs. During that decade of the twittering 'twenties I had often to work through the night on the books and journalism which brought in the money necessary to enjoy the privilege of living on a small island away from the self-conscious and contrived excitement of that febrile decade. My cats gave me the company I needed at night to fight against the temptation of going to bed. I look back to the joyful relief of six o'clock of a fine summer morning and getting out of my chair in which I had been writing sometimes for as much as nine hours without leaving it, and to asking my cats if they wanted to come for a walk. I see them now uncurling from various cushions all over the room and after a harmony of graceful stretches leading the way out. Outside the walled garden they stop to ask whether I am going round the island on the east side which looks across the sea to Sark with one dark menacing rock between called La Pute Noire (the black harlot) or whether we shall take the westerly path and look across those rock-infested three miles of sea to Guernsey.

"Into the sun's eye," I tell them, turning to the left, and the cats twitching their tails in agreement with the direction turn with me. We pause for a moment by the old privateer's gun which had been mounted where it was since the Napoleonic Wars. I fancy that old privateer made more money out of smuggling brandy from France to England than from harassing French ships. He built himself a house on Jethou some of the rooms of which were papered with banknotes, according to local tradition. The house was already a ruin when I came to the island but I have one of his silver spoons on the handle of which 'Jethou' is engraved.

In due course we would come to a little wood of wind-dwarfed oaks and beeches, the trunks of which were covered so thickly with lichen to protect themselves against the salty air that the smooth bark of the beeches was indistinguishable from the rugged trunks of the oaks. On this morning at May's end the ground below would not be visible under a hyacinthine mist of bluebells, but the hoop-petticoat daffodils that grow by the edge of the wood in April would have left us until another year. It was considered my duty to sit for awhile and allow the cats time to explore the wood. This had to be done with as much caution as a jungle full of wild animals would have demanded. After a few minutes during which not one of the cats caught even a butterfly we would walk on round the southerly slopes of the island, pink and white with thrift and campion. The cats might have stalked some of the wrens which often nested in the clumps of butcher's broom if they had not been assailed by the herring-gulls whose eggs were numerous on the rocky steps that led down to the sea's edge. The cats would trot along in single file (one of the characteristics of the Siamese cat is its trot) their ears low until we had passed the gulls' territory and were among the great granite boulders on the westerly slopes. Here I would rest again to allow the cats to indulge in a little mountaineering until they and I felt it was time for porridge. The northerly slope above the garden was a hawthorn wood with ancient Spanish chestnuts and pear-trees and one magnificent ash. This must have been planted at the same time as the great mulberry-tree in the garden over two hundred years ago. I have seen nowhere in the islands round the coast of Great Britain a wood of comparable impressiveness so close to the sea. Coffee would be ready by the time we reached the house, and while I drank mine the cats would have a long drink of water. Siamese cats never take milk for refreshment; in fact they only really enjoy it when they can jump up on the tea-table and drink it from the milk-jug or from the glass upon a bedside table. For that matter they enjoy water much more if they can drink it out of a carafe on the drinks table. This seems to have the same effect on water for them as adding whisky to it has for us.

With the coffee came my porridge, and there was also porridge for the cats. All our kittens were brought up on it and although as they grew older they ceased to accept porridge as a staple dish they never entirely lost a taste for it on occasions. I have already mentioned their passion for prawns. To this can be added lobster, and in the case of Sylvia pâté de foie gras. Their favourite birds were woodcock and golden plover; snipe with infallible good taste they did not care for.

However, on Jethou rabbit was always the main dish of the day and apart from the cooked rabbit they hunted for themselves they ate innumerable rabbits raw. I spoke just now of infallible good taste in not liking snipe. I cannot congratulate my cats on this zest for rabbit. To my taste it is the most unpleasant food that can be offered. My notion of hell in the way of food is a perpetual diet of rabbit and parsnips.

After breakfast in those days of very hard work I used to retire to bed and sometimes sleep until four o'clock in the afternoon. At last the need to gather in every pound my pen could earn became less pressing and those nights did not have to be so long. Looking back on them, I can declare that without that tranquil company of cats by which I was surrounded and the prospect of that early morning walk I should have lacked the will-power to stick it. As I called each one's name, however deep seemed their repose, ears would twitch and tails would quiver, and instead of being left to wrestle with one confounded sentence after another alone I became a member of that tranquil company.

After 1925 I was spending more and more time in Scotland every year and in 1930 when the opportunity came I decided to leave Jethou and live on an island in the Inverness-shire river Beauly instead. My cats were to become Thailanders.

Thailanders

THERE can be very few houses so romantically situated as Eilean Aigas. It was built by the present Lord Lovat's great-grandfather for that strange pair of eccentric visionaries known as the Sobieski Stuarts who believed that they were the direct descendants of Prince Charles Edward Stuart, and indeed managed to convince many of the Inverness-shire lairds that their claim was well founded. They used to be rowed along the river in a kind of state barge to hear Mass in Eskadale church in which I inherited their pew, the only really luxurious pew I have known, with cushions of crimson velvet to kneel on instead of hassocks.

The island was reached by a bridge under which the Beauly went foaming to flow calmly round one side of it beside low banks covered with lilies-of-the-valley in their season. On the other side below sheer cliffs of considerable height the river foamed through a ravine towards the bridge. The island itself was covered with great larches and many other trees. The capercailzie nested there; brown squirrels abounded; in winter the crossbills were a delight to watch.

On the morning after the Thailanders arrived they all came rushing into the house in a panic, their fur bristling and their tails like bottle brushes. I asked them what on earth was the matter, and was told in something between a mew and a sob that a terrible monster was coming up the drive. Nothing would persuade them to come with me when I went to investigate.

The terrible monster proved to be a horse bringing up a load of wood. None of the cats had ever seen a horse. Nor for that matter had they ever seen a motor-car. Machinery, however, in any shape did not alarm them because they had been used to the dynamo which gave us our electricity on Jethou. So when they met their first motor car they thought it was just a good shelter for them to lie under. I teased the cats about their panic over a horse, and at last managed to persuade Stumps to come out and watch me pat it.

"You see, there was nothing to be frightened of. A horse! My goodness, how the cats on Herm would have laughed at you. They weren't even frightened of our bull. And we had a pretty fierce ram who once charged our shepherd twice round the house. Yes, you'd all have been the laughing-stock of the Herm cats for being frightened by a horse."

By this time Stumps had recovered his voice and in his deepest miaows he protested that the Herm cats had been familiar with horses since they were kittens and that if the Herm cats had met a horse for the first time when they were grown up they too would probably have panicked.

"I see now that we were mistaken. Even I was mistaken," Stumps mewed.

And at the thought of such an almost unimaginable state of affairs his double-kinked tail twitched and quivered in astonishment.

At the same time I could see that Stumps was mortified. He could not jeer at Baron or Bimbo or Boy for their cowardice because he knew that he had been as much of a coward himself. I could see by his effort to look unself-conscious when his mother's arrogant blue eyes were on him that he felt he had disappointed her. It would be idle for him to remind her that she had run away from the sight of that horse as fast as himself. Those arrogant blue eyes would narrow contemptuously and convey by their expression that she had a right to do anything she felt like doing.

For some days Stumps brooded over his loss of face. Then one afternoon he met a sheep and that frightened him almost as much as the horse. I met him hurrying up the drive, ears and tail drooping, behind him a sheep which had wandered over the bridge. And I laughed at him. All cats hate to be laughed at, but no cats hate it quite as much as Siamese. Stumps stopped.

"You're laughing at me," he said.

"I am indeed."

"Well, I don't care what big unknown animal I meet next I am not going to be frightened by it."

And I laughed again at his indignant deep miaows.

A week or so later I had gone out to salute the new moon when I heard a deep muffled miaow, and there was Stumps coming along with a polecat in his mouth.

" After all, I *am* somebody."

" Be quick, child. I want to get back to somewhere comfortable."

In the dusk it looked half as big as himself. Then he dropped it and looked up at me to say:

"You thought I was a coward. Merely because I was astonished to see first a horse and then a sheep you thought I should be frightened of any animal I saw for the first time. Well, you were wrong. I don't know what this creature is that I've killed, but he reminded me of our ferrets on Jethou. Except that of course he's a great deal bigger. And when I jumped on him he bit my paw. He made a mistake when he did that because I caught him by the back of his neck and I didn't let go till he was dead."

I bent down to pat my congratulations.

"I expect you'd like to bring your kill into the house and show it to the others," I suggested.

"I certainly should."

"It's a bit of a mouthful. Would you like me to carry it in for you?"

But this offer was rejected and as I put out my hand to pick up the polecat Stumps fixed his teeth in its neck and half-dragged half-carried it in to show all of us, cats and humans, of what prowess he was capable.

His brothers looked on in almost obsequious amazement as Stumps stood growling over his prey.

"Don't dare to come and sniff it, any of you," he growled. "Not one of you would have had the guts to tackle a brute like this."

At this moment Stumps saw his mother's eyes on him.

"Not one of you," he repeated, "except of course mother, only I think he would have been too big for you to tackle, mother. Look where he bit my paw, I tell you, I really did have a fight for it before I killed him."

"Is it good to eat?" Baron asked with a gentle mew.

"Even if it was," Stumps growled at his brother, "I wouldn't let you eat it. This isn't a baby rabbit, which is all you can kill."

Baron mewed sadly. He had not yet been able to find a baby rabbit on Eilean Aigas.

In the early spring of 1931 Sylvia was involved in a disreputable affair with a black cat, the offspring of which made their mark in Inverness-shire. Sylvia's sons were rather upset by mother's lapse but none of them had the courage to tell her so and her dignity was unimpaired. Nevertheless, I felt it was a bad precedent and the next time she proclaimed her desire for matrimony she was sent

7

south to a former husband. The result was that in the summer of her tenth year she produced a litter of eight male kittens.

I have no access to the records of cat breeders but I imagine that such an event must be extremely rare. It was easy to find homes for so many male kittens. One of them, who was called Peter, joined the other Thailanders.

Grigi, Rum and Eigg

IN 1931 I was elected Rector of Glasgow University and at the beginning of my
second year of office after the publication of my third volume of war memoirs
I was prosecuted under the Official Secrets Act. This was a bad financial set-
back, for although the fine was a mere £100 the book was suppressed and what
with one thing and another this farcical prosecution cost me nearly £5,000.

This made it imperative for me to start working again as hard as in the earlier
days of Jethou, and I went to live in a cottage on Barra in the Outer Hebrides,
having fallen in love with the island when I had visited it first five years earlier
and returned there several times. I gave up living in Eilean Aigas but left behind
Nellie Boyte in the gardener's cottage to look after the cats.

In the cottage was a small grey tabby, called Grigi. She had been just a cat
about the place until Christina MacSween, my other secretary, and I came to the
cottage and it was remarkable how quickly she responded to intelligent conversation.

During the last twenty years the cat has recovered the esteem in which it was
held until the Victorian spirit made an idol of the dog. It is significant that the
dog has provided no great stories like Dick Whittington and his Cat or Puss in
Boots. In the Nursery Rhymes, too, the cat always has precedence.

"Pussy cat, pussy cat, where have you been?
I've been to London to see the Queen."

An idea grew up that cats preferred places to people, and those who could win
the easy flattery of a dog were baffled by the failure of most cats to respond
immediately to patronage.

"Cats are so selfish. Cats think only of their own comfort. Cats are not affectionate. Cats are so cruel. Cats are such thieves . . ." And on it goes: the comment

of the empty human mind that can only think in banalities oft heard and oft repeated.

Siamese cats were regarded as exceptions and praised because they had canine qualities. The only dogs whose qualities they share are Chows and Pekinese and that is because Chows and Pekinese have feline qualities. At last more and more people are realizing that many of the qualities they admire in Siamese exist in ordinary cats if they take the trouble to bring out those qualities. But they must win the cat's respect and love; they must not wait for the cat to make the first approach, because if they do nine times out of ten they will wait in vain. I can call a noctambulant cat on the other side of a London street and it will cross over to have a brief colloquy with me, but those able to do this are in a small minority.

Grigi, that small grey tabby, astonished Ruairidh Dubh (dark Roderick), the owner of the cottage, by her response to the novel attention paid to her. Then finding that if he paid her attention she would presently respond to his advances Ruairidh became immensely proud of Grigi and would boast about her intelligence at the least excuse. He started talking to her in Gaelic and declared she followed what he was saying better in Gaelic than in English. He was proud too of the way Grigi would go fishing in the burn and hook the small fish out with her paw. Then one day she hooked an eel and Ruairidh was prouder of her than ever.

That summer Grigi produced two kittens, one a tabby, the other a tortoiseshell. We called them Rum and Eigg. They were born in the small sitting-room in which I worked almost incessantly for fifteen months, and once again delight in the company of a cat and of kittens growing into cats sustained my spirit. In due course Eigg was given to an old crofter who lived alone and felt that Eigg was the companion he needed. With him she lived happily and was a comfort to his loneliness.

In the following year I was asked to lecture in Buenos Aires, Montevideo and Rio de Janeiro, and Christina MacSween took Rum to live with her mother in Tarbert in the island of Harris before she joined my wife and myself to make the trip to South America. Rum became devoted to Mrs. MacSween who used to feed her with raw eggs and cream, a dish Rum loved. Every Sunday she would walk to church with Mrs. MacSween and when she saw across the loch the congregation coming out she would walk round to meet her on her way home.

Rum had one taste in food which within my experience is unique. She had what amounted to a passion for melons. She would growl more loudly over a slice of melon than a captured mouse, and she would not leave a fragment of the rind. She had developed this taste as a kitten and kept it to the end of her days when like so many much loved cats and dogs she was killed by a wretched car. Eigg could never understand her sister's taste for melon. She used to sit and gaze in perplexity at Rum growling over her slice. Once she tried a bit of melon herself and shuddered with disgust. I have known a dog who liked grapes and gooseberries: he used to gather the latter from bushes himself. My thrush of whom I wrote earlier liked treacle, but I have never known a cat or dog or bird who liked melons. I tried Rum with other fruit, but without success.

We did not meet any particularly remarkable cats in South America, and for a year after we came back we lived in another Barra cottage without cats until the house I was building was ready. Then it was time for the Thailanders to rejoin us.

The Thailanders Again

I HAD been parted from Sylvia for two and a half years and I decided that it would be wiser to let her stay with Mrs. Hindley in the south of England where her last husband was living. She was now approaching her fourteenth year and I supposed she would not have much longer to live. How wrong I was! She reached the great age of twenty-two in complete possession of her faculties to the last.

My first Sylvia, alas, never reached full maturity. Had she not died young I am positive she would have become as remarkable a personality as my second Sylvia. The latter became a matriarch in the grand style like Queen Victoria; when young she was more comparable with Catherine the Great of Russia.

Suidheachan, the house in Barra, was 'occupied' on November 30th 1935, which as well as being the festival of St. Andrew was also my thirtieth wedding anniversary. After Christmas Stumps, Baron, Bimbo, Boy and Peter arrived from Eilean Aigas. It was a formidable journey for cats. There was first the drive from Beauly to Inverness. Then came the long train journey from Inverness to Kyle of Lochalsh. Finally there was the voyage from Kyle of Lochalsh to Loch Boisdale in South Uist where they had to be transferred to the boat from Castlebay in Barra. It was decided to screw up each cat in a box so that Nellie Boyte who was escorting them could speak words of encouragement through the ventilating holes without being tempted by their protests to undo a basket. They reached Castlebay upon what by good fortune was a calm January midnight. When at last they reached Suidheachan and were released from their boxes the noise of all five of them complaining of the intolerable discomfort in which they had spent the long hours of their journey was terrific. Even Baron's usually gentle mew was almost shrill. However, the dish of rabbit prepared for them acted as a soft pedal, and when this was followed by an introduction to the Aga the discomfort of the journey was forgotten. They had slept in front of open fires. They had slept against radiators. They had slept on chairs just vacated by the human beings who had been sitting in them. But fires went out. Radiators sometimes gurgled unpleasantly. Chairs grew cool. The top of the Aga always provided the same equable warmth under a folded blanket. For the next eight or nine years the Aga was a friend that never failed them. Only Boy did not live long to enjoy it. About a year after the Thailanders came to Barra he was choked in climbing over a wire fence and buried beside the Minch. When their turn came his brothers would lie there too. It was an appropriate resting place, for all of them had been born beside that southern Minch called La Manche. There was no doubt that those cats whose youth had been spent on Jethou welcomed marine surroundings again after the five years they had spent inland. The house was built on a narrow part of the *machair* between the Atlantic about three hundred yards to the west and the Minch which at high tide was hardly thirty yards away. I ought to explain that *machair* is the Gaelic word for the stretches of fine turf that run the whole length of the Outer Hebrides where they face the Atlantic. The soil of the *machair* is sandy and indeed where we lived almost pure sand. There were plenty of rabbits and good pasturage for cattle and Barra ponies. By now the cats were used to horses and not at all disturbed by the antics of the ponies who ran wild and at one time were much sought after by Highland sportsmen.

Prawns were scarce on Barra, but cockles were abundant. Indeed, at low tide there was well over half a square mile of strand composed entirely of cockles and the remains of cockles. There was no cover to stalk small birds, and the only excitement the cats could enjoy in that way was to sit in the library and chatter at the starlings tobogganing down the skylight on their backs.

None of us likes seeing a bird caught by a cat, but the most ruthless behaviour of a cat with its prey is tender compared with that of which a falcon is capable. One of those starlings was caught by a merlin which carried its victim to an angle of the house and I happened to look out of my study-window as the beautiful little fiend was pulling out the starling's tongue. My old friend James Robertson Justice who is a passionate falconer tried to persuade me that I was mistaken but the merlin was on the ground hardly six feet away from the window and as I write these words I can recall exactly the look in its cold adamantine eyes. I wish that cats would not catch birds or play with mice, but so long as human beings hunt stags and foxes I shall not be able to feel acutely shocked by the cruelty of a cat. As for falconry, the behaviour of that merlin may have been exceptional.

The Thailanders were less inclined to go for long walks when they came to live on Barra than once upon a time on Jethou, and unlike so many middle-aged men they were not troubled by that itch for exercise. I do not believe that if cats played golf they would play much golf after they were ten years old, the equivalent of fifty in a human being. They would make desultory excursions on the chance of catching an odd rabbit, but as those merely involved sitting patiently above a rabbit hole they put no strain on their energy.

About eight one morning in the middle of the war I heard Stumps growling outside my bedroom door, followed immediately afterwards by a tap. To my " come in " there came in the skipper of a Norwegian merchant ship, and behind him was his crew. They had been torpedoed out in the Atlantic and in a couple of the ship's boats they had rowed for five days and nights to reach land at last three hundred yards from our house. The cats had to vacate the Aga earlier than usual that morning so that we could give the crew breakfast, and after five days and nights in the Atlantic that breakfast must have tasted pretty good.

The next excitement was the wreck of the *S.S. Politician*. Mr. Thomas Johnston, the Secretary of State for Scotland, had been disturbed by the bombing of a distillery at Leith and decided that as much as possible of the precious whisky which was bringing in so many much needed dollars must be sent out of the country to America. So the *Politician* which was loading a cargo for Jamaica on the Mersey was told to prepare to receive whisky instead and to carry on from Kingston to an American port. She missed the first turning to the left south of Barra, took the second turning between Barra and South Uist instead and on a calm night in a fog landed on a rock in the little harbour of Eriskay, the most welcome visitor to that island since Prince Charles Edward Stuart on a July day in 1745.

As soon as the news reached Barra of the cargo to be salvaged there was no lack of volunteers for the task. Almost every night for many weeks volunteers would be calling at Suidheachan to fortify themselves for the row across to Eriskay with tea and to fortify us on the way back with bottles of whisky. At one time there was a serried row of whisky bottles above my book shelves, a hundred of them or more. Those were noble times for hospitality. Airmen of every

" I'm *not* affected, just dignified."

" Aren't I dignified too? "

rank would be landing on the cockle strand and look in on their way to the radar station further along the west coast.

"You'll have a whisky, Air Marshal?" (or Group Captain or Wing Commander or any other rank).

"Can you spare it?"

"Of course."

And the astonishment with which he gazed at the powerful dram poured out for him was a joy to see.

The cats who did not understand why people enjoyed whisky did not like being disturbed on the Aga by nocturnal visitors and did not share our regrets when the Excise stepped in and sank the *Politician* to make Davy Jones a present of many thousands of cases of whisky. When I came to live in Edinburgh over ten years later an old friend in Barra sent me the last bottle of ' Polly ' he had left with which to drink the health of my new abode.

That whisky galore made up for an earlier disappointment I had had over a wreck. One night a big Greek merchant ship struck a rock on the east side of the island and the Captain hearing I lived on Barra drove round to call on me.

After supper and a long talk of stirring times in Greece during the First World War the Captain, a man of Andros, said when he took his leave,

"This is a very lucky wreck for you, because I will send you olive oil, currants, raisins, almonds, ouzo, retzina, all the things you like in Greece. You will have enough for the whole of this war."

But while we were at supper the ship broke in half, and the half which contained all those things I liked in Greece went down. Next day the Captain came to tell me the sad news.

"But I have brought you a sheep," he said. "That is all I have left of my stores."

That thin black-faced sheep like a coal coming to Newcastle did not compensate me for what had been wasted upon the fishes.

Stumps, Baron and Bimbo were quite fearless with strangers, but Peter was inclined to stage an elaborate panic when he saw them. When a Siamese cat is subject to these panics it is almost impossible to cure it. Two or three people are accepted as friends and the rest of the world are its potential enemies. Whenever Peter did anything wrong he used to retire under the refrigerator in the kitchen and accuse himself with loud miaows of having transgressed. He had nothing to fear in the way of punishment, but he seemed to be driven by a sense of guilt into self-denunciation. I fancy he derived a kind of pleasure from it. If Buchmanship existed in the feline world Peter would have been a great exponent of moral rearmament.

Baron was the second of the Thailanders to leave us. One evening in his nineteenth year he came into the library and talked for a long time with that gentle mew of his. He was always an extremely affectionate cat but on this evening he was more than usually demonstrative, rubbing himself against me and purring and gently mewing. At last he went to the door and when I opened it for him he went a little way along the passage and then came back to rub himself against me once more and, as it seemed, to assure me in gentle mews how fond he was of us all. Then slowly he walked away to take his place on the Aga, as we supposed. Instead he must have gone out of the window which was left open in the passage on the other side of the house. The next morning we found him under the car in the garage, dead. I am convinced that Baron knew he was going to die and that these gentle mews were his way of telling us how much he had enjoyed his life with us, how much he wished he was young again and able to sit all day above a rabbit-hole waiting for baby rabbits to come out, and how sorry he was that the end of his happy life was now at hand. The end may have come when he was asleep because he was lying stretched out under the car in an attitude of perfect serenity. From the time he first met a motor-car after he left Jethou Baron had never lost an opportunity of sitting under a stationary car.

Stumps followed his younger brother a few months later. Alas, he was afflicted at the end with fits and he had to be put away. Bimbo outlived Peter, who died in early middle age, and spent the last two years of his long life with a widow.

Edward

M Y wife had a maisonette above one of the shops in Connaught Place before we bought a cottage in Hampstead's Vale of Health, and it was there that Edward spent his kittenhood. His favourite game was to hide in a clothes-basket that stood in the passage at the top of the stairs while I had to come up slowly calling "Edward" so that when I arrived at the top he could spring out, dance three times round his tail, and then tear down to the bottom of the stairs. It was now my turn to hide. I could not get into the clothes-basket, but I could crouch behind it. Edward would then very cautiously creep upstairs again and when I sprung out at him he would jump into the clothes-basket and I would have to go downstairs for him to spring out at once when I reached the top. He never tired of this game.

During the first years of the war Edward remained in the Vale of Health with a Russian friend and his youthful high spirits were for ever spoilt by the blitz. When he came to live at Denchworth Manor after the war he would be friends with nobody except Christina MacSween, I could not make the slightest impression on him. I was ill for half of 1946 and wrote most of *Whisky Galore* in bed, in a good deal of pain. However, by the autumn I was well enough to go to India, having been invited by the Indian Government to write about the mighty achievement of the Indian Army during the war. This meant travelling all over North Africa, the Near East, the Middle East, India, Nepal, Burma, Malaya and the Far East, the Seychelles and Kenya. We were away for all but four months of two years.

At Flagstaff House in Bolarum the Siamese cats belonging to Brigadier Martin jumped down from a sofa and came across the room to greet me. I was told he did not remember their ever doing that before.

"They must have realised they were greeting their President," I suggested.

59

A week before writing of that visit to Bolarum I received a letter from Portugal addressed to *Sir Compton Mackenzie, President of the Cats Club, England.* The Post Office are wonderful when they have a teaser like that, and the letter was delivered in Edinburgh without delay.

Our host in Singapore was the late Major-General L. H. Cox, and here at Draycot House I saw the only half-breed I have seen with almost perfect Siamese points. A white blotch on her nose and two white paws with a black spot were all that marked a *mésalliance.* Every other Siamese half-breed within my experience has had green or yellow eyes, none blue, with sometimes the characteristic large ears of the Siamese, sometimes the close fine silky fur and, until the determined breeding out of the kinked tail, often a stumpy kinked tail or no tail at all. All the Malay cats I saw had short kinked stumpy tails, and if the theory be correct that the royal Siamese cats were an exclusive inbred strain from ordinary jungle cats of semi-albino cats designed to receive the souls of members of the royal family for their next transmigration, the influence of the short stumpy tail is naturally powerful. I have already put forward this jungle cat origin as a possible explanation of the Manx cat. I knew a half-Persian half-Siamese cat whose tail was a small fan of fur. We have within recent years been meeting Burmese cats. I have not had the pleasure of knowing a Burmese cat well but their close kinship with Malay and Siamese cats is obvious.

One more observation about Siamese half-breeds. Whatever various physical characteristics they may inherit from their Far Eastern ancestry to a greater or lesser degree, they always within my experience inherit the Siamese character and temperament. Finally there is always a risk in the mating of an ordinary Tom with a Siamese queen, and I have known of several cases of death in parturition because the bone structure of our domestic cat is larger and tougher than the bone structure of a Siamese.

I have already mentioned the ginger Siamese cat with whom I made friends at the Bangkok aerodrome. Later on at the hotel I made friends with a dark grey cat who was very conversational. But the most typical encounter with a Siamese cat was in the enchanted enclosure of the Temple of the Reclining Buddha. In the course of exploring this wonderland at sunset we found what looked like a small temple with a placard outside to say that donations were welcome. I presented some Malay dollars to an ancient monk in his chrome-yellow robe and expressed a desire to see inside the temple. When the door was opened a black and white cat sprang out with loud Siamese miaows to demand a reason for her incarceration in what seemed to be a cross between a library and a large box-room presided over by a small gilded Buddha. Nevertheless, in spite of her indignation, she was willing to escort us round, but when the monk suggested that she should be locked up again inside she refused, with a yowl of outraged protest. The monk explained to her that it was her duty to deal with the rats. She rubbed herself against me and in a string of miaows asked me to tell the monk that she was not willing to spend a dark, lonely and uncomfortable night by killing rats for human beings whose religion did not allow them to kill rats themselves. I gave the old monk another dollar.

"Let her stay outside."

He smiled and shut the temple door to the obvious relief of the black and white cat who thanked me and wandered off among the slim pagodas covered with porcelain mosaic in exquisite pastel shades. Dusk was deepening fast, and it would have been useless to take advantage of the monk's offer to unlock the Temple of the Reclining Buddha, for the interior would have been dark. So the monk blessed us before we said farewell, asking for us a happy life.

Over ten years have passed since I heard the indignant miaows of that black and white cat in that Thailand temple enclosure, but I can still hear them with the mind's ear. At the time they brought back the voices of my own Thailanders, all of them by now safe in that Elysium where cats of character sleep for ever among the asphodels.

Edward was happy to see Christina again when we returned to Berkshire in May 1948, but he was still a solitary and gloomy cat and his sole happiness was when bedtime came and he could retire to sleep every night with the only person he cared for except the Russian friend with whom he had spent those terrifying nights in Hampstead during the war. Tried I ever so hard he would not make friends with me. The memory of those games with the clothes-basket he used to play with me as a kitten had been obliterated by the noise of bombs. About two years after our return from the East Edward fell ill and it was necessary to have him put away.

My wife had a stuffed Tom tabby cat who had lived through the siege of Sebastopol where he had been rescued by some of our soldiers and brought back to England. He was an exceptionally large cat and he may now be seen in the museum of the R.M.A. at Sandhurst.

No Cats About the House

AFTER the death of Edward I decided against having another Siamese cat at Denchworth. I did not believe that Denchworth would be our final abode and was only waiting until I could find the right surroundings in Scotland for books and cats before I left it. When that happened it would be time to have a cat again. Nellie Boyte had a large neuter tabby called Poodge; he was a wise and dignified animal and his death was a great grief to all.

I take this opportunity to preach a little sermon. If anybody makes up his mind to own a Siamese cat he must make up his mind at the same time to be owned by the cat. There is no point in having a Siamese cat unless one is prepared in the eyes of the world to spoil it. Unfortunately too many people nowadays acquire a Siamese cat because so many other people do. Such people are not qualified to be entrusted with a Siamese cat. For my part I strongly object to people who keep an old-fashioned tabby as a kitchen appendage. However, this tiresome habit is so engrained that it is a waste of eloquence and emotion to try to cure people of it. The damnable folk who go away for their summer holidays and leave their cat behind in some respectable suburb think that if they ask a neighbour to put some food and milk in the potting shed for the animal they have left behind they have done all that can be expected of them.

"Cats are always much fonder of a place than they are of the people in it," they will say with that fatuous complacency of the stereotyped mind.

Sometimes the neighbour feeds the cat; sometimes it does not. Cats are not scavengers like dogs, and to drive a cat into scavenging is a sin against nature. I am strongly in favour of making a cat's licence compulsory like a dog's. Yet for reasons I am unable to follow the cat fancy as a whole have always opposed a licence for cats.

Siamese cats are not left behind when their owners go away for the summer holidays. Why? Because people have usually had to pay for the pleasure of feeling fashionable in the ownership of a Siamese cat and so it is provided for in absence. I maintain that to charge cat owners even the inadequate 7s. 6d. that a dog licence costs would make them better aware of their responsibility.

However, although people with Siamese cats do not disgracefully abandon them to suit their own convenience, far too many of them are quite unworthy of the privilege of keeping a Siamese cat. They do not realize that Siamese cats must be 'spoilt' if their owners wish to get the best out of them, or indeed anything at all out of them. Nobody who understands and loves Siamese will disagree with that statement. If you meet a dull Siamese in a household you may be sure that the people are dull in the opinion of their cat. Dogs and Siamese cats get on together well if the dog accepts the fact of the cat's superior status in the household, and this an intelligent dog will always do. But if the members of the household pay an exaggerated attention to the dog the cat will despise them for it and will often desert that household as unworthy of its patronage. I have known several instances of this.

"Cats are so selfish. Cats think only of their own comfort. Cats have no loyalty. Cats have no affection . . . " and so on and so on.

Let it be granted at once that the dog will pander to its master's weaknesses by a demonstrative display of its dependence upon that master, but let it also be granted that the love of a dog is immensely much easier to win than the love of a cat. The personal relationship between Siamese cats and the man or woman who understands them often tempts the visitor to observe that Siamese cats are more like dogs under the impression that he is paying his host's cat a great compliment. Those who acquire Siamese cats because they think they will behave like dogs are in for a disappointment. A dog is never demanding: it responds to the demands of its master. Siamese cats are the most demanding animals in the world, and unless you are prepared to surrender to those demands it will be wiser not to keep a Siamese cat. I have seen many performing cats in circus shows but I have never seen Siamese cats perform and I question the ability of anybody to train them to perform. Lion-taming would be an easy job compared with that.

I regret that I have never enjoyed an intimate friendship with one of the large cats. I envy those who have been on familiar terms with a lion or a leopard. I met a cheetah once, and I have never been more gratified than when this great lovely cat rolled over and purred when I scratched it under the chin. A friend of mine in Burma once had a leopardess who slept at the foot of his bed for over two years. Then one day when he was being attentive to the little daughter of a high official he noticed a look in Ruth's eyes (Ruth was the name of the leopardess) which made him think she was about to spring. He caught her quickly by the collar, but he felt he could not risk having her loose about the house any more, and so he presented her to the Rangoon Zoo. He used to visit her every day but she pined for him too much when he was away and a fortnight later she died of grief.

I think one would probably have to be a bachelor to win the devotion of a great cat. Siamese cats are intensely jealous, but their jealousy is manageable. A jealous lioness or leopardess would be another matter.

I have read several accounts of lion cubs growing up as domestic pets but I fancy that they always have to be banished soon after they are full grown.* My friend's leopardess is the first I have heard of as a friend of man. Lion-taming and tiger-taming disgust me because I believe the relationship is based on fear, not upon affection, and if I had my way I would make performing tigers and lions illegal entertainment.

I have been told that the puma makes friends easily with man but I have never heard that the other great South American cat, the jaguar, was capable of domestic behaviour. Our own wild cat in Scotland can never be tamed. The kittens will spit and growl at a human being as soon as their eyes are open. And the offspring of a union between a wild cat and a domestic cat that has run wild are equally savage. I have only once seen a genuine wild cat in Scotland and that was in Glen Affric in the days before hydro-electric development. It crossed the road in front of the car and went bounding up the brae on the other side, turning round about twenty yards up to curse us. I was telling this story to my companion in a jeep when driving through the jungle from Kalewa to Pyangaing in Burma and saying I did not suppose I should have the luck to see a leopard, and as I finished speaking a leopardess with her cub crossed the road and plunged up the slope of the jungle. This is an unusual sight in the daytime.

* When I wrote those words the story of Elsa the lioness had not been published. *Born Free* by Joy Adamson has been a revelation. To Elsa I have dedicated *Cats' Company*.

"These ordinary cats are very nice when you get to know them."

" Am I to be kept sitting on this cold linoleum for ever? "

" Well, tabby cats can hide their claws. We Siamese can't."

" I think there's somebody at the front door."

" Do pretend to be frightened, mother."

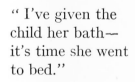

" I've given the child her bath— it's time she went to bed."

That's enough about the great cats. I have no more chance of keeping one in Edinburgh than I should have of keeping a giraffe, which is an animal to which I have been greatly attracted ever since one leant over its railings at the Zoo nearly seventy years ago and pulled some of the flowers out of the hat our strict governess was wearing.

During the years I was without the company of cats I was never for a moment tempted to get a dog. There have been only two dogs in my life to which I have been deeply attached. These were the bulldog Smut whom I mentioned earlier and an Old English sheepdog called Bob whom we had in Burford and Cornwall and who came to live with my publisher Martin Secker at Iver when we went to Italy. I recognize the gratification and encouragement that a dog can be to countless men and women but I should derive no comfort from a dog's assurance that I was a wonderful chap. I should regard such an assurance as too easily earned. No man may be a hero to his valet but every man is a hero to his dog. The dog is a romantic; the cat is a realist. That will serve as a rough dichotomy, but it should be added that spaniels are sentimentalists.

The Pekinese and the Chow have as much realism in them as cats. It is significant that the remarkable growth in popular esteem of the cat during the last thirty years has coincided with a decline in humbug. During the Victorian age when Papa's whiskers were the top nobody would have ventured to call somebody or something the cat's whiskers. I cannot trace the phrase beyond 1927 as an expression of praise. One of the tributes to cats I most dislike is to hear them called mysterious. I dislike the word equally as an epithet for women. The behaviour of women is much more surely predictable than the behaviour of men. The only mystery about the cat is to know why it ever decided to become a domestic animal. The most plausible explanation is that the cat once upon a time discovered that man was able to provide it with that comfort which the cat regards as the object of its existence. I detect a parallel to be drawn between the cat's attitude and that of the woman who for the sake of security will tolerate existence with a man whom the rest of his sex regard as intolerable.

The anti-cat party cites this desire for comfort as evidence of the cat's selfishness, but no cat I have known has ever claimed to be an altruist. When it surrenders to love an individual man or woman it is always a possessive love and jealousy is dominant, all the more dominant because it is generally indifferent to human attentions and unprepared to acknowledge them. Dogs are jealous but it is a

9

competitive tail-wagging jealousy without depth of feeling, the sort of jealousy children display when showing off. Of course, there are innumerable exceptions. I have mentioned that Skye terrier whom my mother gave to her sister when she married and who would never speak to her again.

For me one of the pleasures of cats' company is their devotion to bodily comfort. To look up from the sheet of foolscap on which I am struggling to find the right words in the right order and see on the other side of the room a huddle of cats asleep in perfect tranquillity is as restful to my mind as the cushion on which they are lying is restful to their bodies. I feel that to avoid disturbing them I must stick to my work.

Then there is the independence of the cat which is so absurdly resented by the dog lover. I welcome such independence. Mind you, it can be carried much too far by some cats, though I suspect that when it is carried too far the people of the house are to blame because they have failed to convince their cat that they regard it as a friend and not as a mere appendage of the household. Siamese are dependent on human company and they are never contented indoors unless they are in human company. For that matter they are always happier out of doors if people are with them.

If the friends go away for a time no cats, not even Siamese cats, will welcome their return with the faintest effusion. They seem anxious to impress upon the prodigal who has returned that his absence had been unnoticed. The coolness of this reception will last until the regular routine of the household's existence is resumed. Then without any marked demonstration of pleasure the cat will fall in with that routine and merely by doing so convince you as it thinks that it welcomes your return. On the other hand, the dog will greet the returned prodigal with a boisterous display of pleasure. This naturally flatters the prodigal, and the dog's affection for him makes him believe that the dog is more faithful than the cat, and that the welcome he has received proves that the dog is the superior animal. We catlovers cannot argue the point, for if we do we shall be seeming superior by suggesting that we are able to get on without the outward and visible signs of love.

Dog lovers may rightly claim that nobody has a horror of dogs comparable to the horror of cats which affects some people. Anti-dog feeling never reaches further than cold dislike, but horror is not too strong a word for the feeling that cats can excite. How does one account for a man like Lord Roberts shivering with apprehension if a cat was in the room he entered? Was he carried off by a man-eating tiger in a previous incarnation? Was he overlaid by a cat in his cradle? The latter is a favourite explanation for a state of mind frequent enough in maturity. I do not find it a satisfactory explanation. I should have thought that if a baby woke up to find a cat sitting on its head it would be more liable to claustrophobia when grown up than to shuddering at the idea of a cat being in the room.

The strange thing is that if a cat senses antipathy in a person it will deliberately as often as not jump into that person's lap and ignore those present who would be only too flattered if it would jump upon one of their laps. The contrariness of cats is familiar to all who love them, and we discern in such contrariness the cat asserting its individualism and abhorrence of the herd spirit so increasingly noticeable in human beings. It would be in keeping with a cat's character deliberately to choose for its attentions somebody who found them unwelcome. How does the cat pick out in a roomful of people the one person who least wants to be picked out? I leave the question unanswered.

Presumably it was the cat's individualism which led to the notion that it was a spiteful animal. It is significant, however, that it was not until the 'eighties of the last century that 'catty' came into common usage for the veiled malice of feminine comment. The dog was still the noblest animal, at any rate in Britain. It would have been unthinkable then to talk about 'bitchy' behaviour as we do to-day because it would have cast a reflection upon a woman's morals rather than upon her manners. It is significant, too, that from the time when dog-worship began to decline a genteel euphemism like 'lady dog' became non-U. Let me add that I am not suggesting that people to-day are any less fond of dogs than they used to be in the Victorian age; it is merely that romanticism is out of fashion. There still exist hobbledehoy oafs who think it clever to set their dogs to chase cats in the back gardens of subtopia, but they are frowned upon by the great majority of their neighbours, and I observe among the children of to-day as much regard for the cat as for the dog. This was certainly not the case in my boyhood when excessive devotion to a cat was often regarded with suspicion as a sign of 'cissiness'. If Dick Whittington had turned again on Highgate Hill to become a Victorian lord mayor, he would have arrived back in London Town with a dog.

The stimulus I receive from the company of cats is their unflagging curiosity.

The lesson is constant, and as I regard the preservation of curiosity as one of the great prophylactics against the dangerously sedative influence of old age I rejoice in the tonic example set by cats. Not a drawer can be pulled out but a cat must investigate its contents. It knows that it will probably find the usual collection of shirts or socks or handkerchiefs from which the wash has removed every interesting smell, but it will still investigate on the chance of discovering a novelty. Eldorado calls to it as long ago it called to Raleigh. Those who are considering the introduction of a Siamese cat to their house will do well to remember that Siamese are much more restless than Persian, half-Persian and ordinary cats. Siamese always have a perfectly clear idea of what they want whether it be a particular chair, a particular dish or a particular room. Therefore people who belong to Siamese cats must make up their minds to do a good deal of waiting upon them. Perhaps the characteristic of cats that many of their lovers find most attractive is their tranquillity. I fear that this tranquillity cannot be claimed for Siamese unless like children they are asleep. They compete with pot-holers and mountaineers in causing immense trouble to other people to extricate them from difficult situations. They are merciless to upholstery. They delight in making one get up from one's chair to let them into a room and then a few minutes later making one get up again to let them out of the room the arrangements of which have failed to suit the mood of the moment. I insist upon this aspect of the Siamese because few things depress me more than the sight of a Siamese cat whose lot has been cast with people unable to understand what it asks from life. Siamese cats are unable to indulge in the self-pity which allays with gentle massage a chip on the shoulder: they are just lonely and dull.

An old friend of mine once decided that he must have a Siamese cat, but neither he nor his wife nor his children have the faintest notion of how to treat a Siamese cat. I knew any advice from me to them would be idle. So I offered it to the cat.

Self.   You're not happy here, are you?

Cat.   Oh, I'm happy enough. I'm well fed. I have plenty of comfortable chairs. The house was cold at first but since this business they call central heating was put in I'm no longer chilly.

Self.   But you're bored.

Cat.   You've said it. I'm bored. Damnably bored.

Self. Yes, I felt that.

Cat. These people are perfectly kind. I've been living with them now for nearly four years. But they are doggy people, and I think they ought to have a dog.

Self. Would you like that?

Cat. No, I shouldn't but it would give me an excuse to leave them if they brought a dog here.

Self. Where would you go?

Cat. There's a woman living about a mile from here whom I visit occasionally. I think it would be a kindness to go and stay with her because she is undoubtedly lonely. I can tell that by the way she talks to me. I'm at my wits' end here for intelligent conversation.

I took an early opportunity of asking my old friend why he did not keep a dog. He told me that there was nothing he would like better but that he was worried about the cat's reaction. A few weeks later however, a golden Labrador puppy arrived, and my friend wrote to tell me that the cat had left them next day and gone to live with an old maid in the neighbourhood. The next time I went to stay with my friend I called on the cat. I asked him if he was happy and was glad to hear that he was.

"But do tell her not to waste milk on me and also to see that there is plenty of water available."

When I returned to Edinburgh I decided that it was high time we had a cat about the house again. The travail of the move from Berkshire was behind us and the presence of workmen was no longer liable to upset a cat. I was offered a Siamese blue-point kitten and in March 1954 Bluebell arrived in Drummond Place.

Bluebell, Pinkibuff and Pippo

I HAD hesitated at first about accepting Bluebell because I had got into my head that blue-points were apt to be nervous, and, as I said before, Siamese kittens who are nervous seldom grow out of it. I need not have worried. Bluebell stepped out of her travelling basket completely calm, completely self-possessed and completely at home. Her late mistress observed that she was longing to be the centre of attention and that she had not been able to give her as much as she wanted because Bluebell's mother demanded so much.

Bluebell gazed at my book-lined study, jumped down from the couch on which she had emerged from her basket and walked round this strange room, noting an occasional gap in the bookshelves as a convenient place to hide if she should think that bedtime had arrived too soon. Then back upon the couch she eyed the people with whom she had come to live and decided that Christina MacSween was the one she could love best, and what was more important by whom she could be loved best. She slept with her that night and from that night she has never sat upon anybody else's lap if Christina's lap was there to be sat on. Indeed, she is very chary of sitting on other people's laps. Two or three of my women friends are occasionally honoured but my men friends never. Against my lap she was immediately prejudiced by what she considered my unpleasant habit of wearing corduroy trousers. However, she discovered that when I am reading my letters and papers in bed my outstretched legs offer exactly the right support for her front paws and she usually spends the rest of the morning with me after I wake up.

Bluebell is not what people call a friendly cat. If strangers lean down to stroke her she quivers with disgust at the familiarity and walks away. Except to her beloved Christina she seldom displays affection. If she is by herself with me and in the mood she can be and indeed usually is demonstrative, but if anybody else

70

comes into the room she at once becomes self-conscious and tries to look as if she was meeting me for the first time.

She is a very dainty cat over food and unlike most Siamese not in the least greedy. Therefore she never indulges in cupboard love, though occasionally when she feels it is time that a fire was lit she will throw herself out at full length to be stroked by Mrs. Sutherland, one of our daily helpers, and try to lure her with purrs into lighting that fire. If the purrs do not produce the fire she will scold Mrs. Sutherland with indignant miaows.

One day Bluebell came along to the door of my study and mewed loudly.

"All right, all right, I'm sorry to have to keep you waiting. I was finishing a sentence."

But she stood by the open door and continued to mew loudly.

"What do you want?"

"Follow me and I'll show you what's the matter."

She went pattering down the passage until she reached the kitchen where the kettle on the stove was on the verge of boiling over.

"How can one eat one's supper with a noise like that going on? It's as bad as that beastly Hoover."

The kettle was silenced and Bluebell went back to her supper.

When the time came for Bluebell to be married we found that a blue-point husband would involve a long journey. So a *marriage de convenance* was arranged with a seal-point close at hand, and in due course she brought two kittens into the world, one male and one female. Both were seal-points, Pinkie being much darker than Pippo, her brother.

It was the little girl next door who called her Pinkie. Feeling that the responsibility of another female cat in the house would be too much for us I had promised to give her to that little girl when she should be six weeks old.

"I shall call her Pinkie."

I said I did not think it was quite an appropriate name for a kitten with eyes like sapphires and a buff coat.

"Wouldn't Pinkibuff be more suitable?" I suggested.

This was accepted, and in due course the six-weeks'-old Pinkibuff was carried away in the arms of her new mistress to the house next door. Forty-eight hours later the little girl returned with Pinkibuff in her arms.

"She hasn't stopped crying for a moment ever since she came to us. And Nanny has a headache and Uncle Jim has a headache and I have a headache. If I pick her up she goes on crying and if I put her down she goes on crying. And she won't eat anything. She just goes on crying. So please I don't think I'll be able to keep her any longer."

The little girl next door was nearly in tears herself and after putting Pinkibuff gently down she hurried away.

The first thing that the kitten did was to go to her plate in the kitchen and eat. Her eyes had been very weak after she was born, but forty-eight hours of crying seemed to have cured the weakness. We felt guilty about the unhappiness to which the wee creature had been subjected and her perfectly obvious relief in being once more with her mother and brother and the people she knew was a reproach to our belief that a six-weeks' old kitten would soon be at home in strange surroundings.

In fact Pinkibuff has never forgotten that experience of hers in early youth, and to-day over four years later she will not let herself be stroked by a little girl and only by a very few exceptional little boys. Two years after her adventure the little girl next door came back to Edinburgh on a visit—her family had moved south. As soon as Pinkibuff heard her voice in the hall she fled for protection to my arms with what was nearly a cry of distress and fear.

If she saw little girls walking past our front door when it was open she would rush in a panic to hide herself. To her little girls were as much of a menace as gypsies used to be to children in the children's books of long ago. Every early Victorian child dreaded being stolen by gypsies, stripped of her clothes, and stained with walnut-juice. Indeed, I must admit that even in the early 'eighties of the last century I was glad that people were about when a gypsy caravan whose inhabitants were hawking brushes and brooms passed down a Kensington street.

I was thankful that Pinkibuff insisted even when she was only six weeks old that we were the only people with whom she wanted to live, for she is as lovable a cat as any of the cats in my life. She was a tiny kitten and is still an unusually small cat, but she keeps in strict order her elder brother, who is half as big again as herself. She is devoted to her mother but she makes it clear to her that she is completely independent of parental control.

Many cats and dogs dislike being stared at by human beings and this may have led to the superstitition that an animal cannot meet the human eye directly and under its gaze will retreat. I call it a superstition because apart from the behaviour of certain dogs and cats I have never found any evidence of its truth.

" Lamplight isn't sunshine, you know."

Pippo, Bluebell, Pinkibuff (reading from left to right)

The author and his cats of the moment writing this book

I should certainly feel extremely doubtful of my own ability to quell a tiger by the fixity of my gaze.

Siamese cats are always able to stare back if they are being stared at but I have never known any cat except Pinkibuff who could sit staring you in the eyes for as long as you were willing to stare back. She has a passion for 'caves', and nothing delights her more than to find a woman visitor with a long skirt under which she will sit in a deep twilight of complacent enjoyment. Her particular favourites for this temporary seclusion from the world are the skirts of nuns which provide her with a darkness much deeper than twilight. She, like her mother, does not talk unless she has really something to say. The other day we were led down to the bottom of the house to be shown where her brother was shut up in a cupboard. Bluebell had been inclined to think that it would do Pippo good to be shut up for an hour or two in a cupboard and had made no attempt to rescue him.

Bluebell had an affair with a local Tom of low origin and produced a litter which she refused to suckle. Pinkibuff was distressed by such parental irresponsibility and although she was hardly six months old at the time she did her best to mother the poor little unwanted ones. Pippo on the other hand spat at them to show what he thought of his mother's disgrace. We had to have them put away by the vet, and I decided to take the risk of making a repetition of such a business impossible.

After losing Venetia I had always refused to let any more of our female kittens be exposed to the danger of the operation. However, it was obviously impossible to keep two female cats in a town house otherwise and I agreed to the operation. It was performed so skilfully by our Edinburgh vet that Bluebell and Pinkibuff seemed unaware that anything had happened, and when the time came for the vet to take the stitches out they let him do it without so much as a twitch. So provided a good vet is available nobody need worry about any risk. I have seen it stated that this operation is apt to change a cat's character and make it dull and eccentric. There is certainly neither dullness nor eccentricity in Bluebell and Pinkibuff.

By an alarming coincidence on the night after I had written during the afternoon the account of the death of my first Sylvia from that foul gastro-enteritis Finkibuff developed a swelling in the throat and I was much upset by the fear that I might be going to lose her. We telephoned to the vet and he came round at 11 p.m. Lily MacSween and I held her while he gave her an injection and gratefully we were able to let him know next morning that she seemed better. It was some kind of glandular infection and she was in pain for several days, but she was completely cured, and my gratitude to that vet is profound.

Pippo is a perfect example of a seal-point Siamese neuter, and I have sometimes thought of entering him in a show to provide him with the attention he feels he should have. As things are he thinks that his mother and his sister steal too much of it. He was upset in adolescence by his mother's unfortunate affair with that local Tom of low origin, and ever since he has waged war on every male intruder into his garden for fear that Bluebell will disgrace him again. What annoys him is that his mother is so extremely west-endy Edinburgh with people who visit the house. Pippo himself is ready to be agreeable to callers. He welcomes the opportunity of displaying his courtly manners, and purrs to hear their comment on his friendliness.

Pippo (to Bluebell).   Can't you be gracious to people who visit us? I hate the way you shudder when somebody bends down to stroke you.

Bluebell.   I am not interested in people who don't belong to us.

Pippo.   That's very evident. But you were interested enough in that ghastly bounder with whom you carried on.

Bluebell.   Please don't remind me of that unfortunate episode. It won't occur again.

Pippo.   I'll jolly well see it doesn't occur again.

Bluebell.   I wasn't enormously impressed by the way you handled that new cat next door. You were sitting opposite on the wall for over an hour and he didn't budge an inch. In the end it was you who jumped off the wall and came into the house with your tail like a bottle brush, looking so fierce. But I noticed you didn't go back on the wall. Instead you sat on Aunt Christina's desk, growling at him from the window of her room. Very brave, I'm sure.

Pippo.   I shall box your ears if you talk to me like that.

And this is usually the end of one of those arguments.

Another thing that Pippo disapproves of in his mother and sister is their extreme daintiness.

Pippo.   Why can't you tuck in the way I do? You both sniff at your food as if it was going to bite you. And then when I can't stand watching your affectation

any longer and eat up what you're both sniffing at you complain to Aunt
Christina that I'm so greedy you don't get a chance to eat your own supper.
And those yeast pills you and Pinkibuff pretend to enjoy so much . . .
Bluebell (interrupting).   They are delicious and they are very good for us.
Perhaps if you chewed up a yeast pill every morning you'd be better able to
deal with this new cat next door who's your own age. There's no glory in
driving poor old broken down Toms out of the garden.
Pippo.   It was a pity you didn't think of that when you let the most disreputable one of the lot make love to you. Anyway, I don't like yeast pills. What's
more I don't believe you and Pinkibuff like them any better than I do. You
pretend to like them just to suck up to Aunt Christina.
Bluebell.   We do like them. You know perfectly well that if Aunt Christina
ever forgets to give them to us we always go up and ask her for them.

This is true. Bluebell and Pinkibuff do not consider their day is complete
without a yeast pill. Pippo gets his too, but it is crumbled over his food so that he
can have the tonic without tasting it. They are all fish-eaters in preference to
anything else. Indeed, none of them is fond of meat except rabbit, and they all
regard fat with as much disgust as most children do.

Mrs. Wood, a famous fishwife, comes from Musselburgh every Thursday and every
Thursday they sit waiting in the hall for her arrival. That really fresh fish makes
up for the arrival on Thursday of the gardener of whose behaviour they all
complain. "The man will interfere with us," we are told. "What are garden-beds
for except for us to scratch in? This morning he has put a lot of wire-netting over
our favourite bed. We'd like to know where he'd be if we didn't chase the birds
out of our garden. He'd have no flowers at all."

I am glad to say that the blackbirds, starlings and sparrows are very seldom
caught. Pippo, however, on two occasions has performed a feat which I should
have supposed was impossible. He has twice caught a swift on the wing as it
swooped down after an insect. On both occasions the feat was seen and the swift
rescued.

Pippo has had only one experience comparable in its anxiety to those forty-
eight hours Pinkibuff spent when we gave her to the little girl next door. It
happened when Christina MacSween and I were away in Greece working on a
television programme. One night he did not come home and when he was still

missing next day Lily MacSween put an advertisement in the paper. A kind woman called on the following evening to say that she had seen a cat like the one described go into a basement cellar in a street about a quarter of a mile away. So Lily set off to find the truant. Black as one of those common cats he so much despised he leapt into her arms when he heard his name called and snuggling into her, his heart beating, he was carried home on a chill November evening. After being cleaned and fed he sat in front of the fire, gazing into it as if to tell it he had despaired of ever seeing a fire again. His mother had spat at him when he came home: presumably he had imported into the house a lot of smells that offended her superior nose. Pinkibuff, however, tried to clean him up.

We never knew how Pippo came to be in that coal cellar. Probably somebody had picked him up when he was wandering around in the tennis-courts at the back of the house and carried him to a strange street. He may have escaped and taken refuge in the cellar. By being carried he would have lost the scent by which he could find his way home, and anyway he is frightened of traffic and would not have dared to cross a road by himself.

Not very long after this escapade of Pippo the much loved cat of a neighbour was killed by a car when crossing the road. No statistics are produced about the deaths of cats and dogs, but when on Christmas Eve 1959 sixty-six human beings were killed by cars the mortality among cats and dogs must have been much higher. What will it be at the end of another decade? Much higher still, and the depressing thought is that no kind of remedy for this state of affairs is even remotely in sight. I can only be thankful that none of our cats has the least desire to wander in the streets. It is always a temptation to take Siamese cats out walking with one, but it is a temptation to be resisted unless they are living on a small island without motor-cars, without traps, without keepers and without thieves, because if a Siamese cat is encouraged to go out when accompanied the moment will come when it will decide to take a walk on its own with perhaps a fatal result.

I have told the story of the cats in my life, and looking back through the years I am more sharply aware than ever how much I owe to them. I like to think that Bluebell, Pinkibuff and Pippo are as happy as cats can possibly be. Only one thing is denied and that is the freedom of the hairdressing salon we have opened in our basement. They cannot understand why they are not allowed to sit and watch ladies under the driers, and Pippo who takes a delight in running water particularly resents not being allowed to watch the shampooing. We have explained to them that there are ladies who do not like cats but they think that this is just a poor excuse to deny them the gratification of their curiosity, and all of them take the first opportunity that occurs of slipping into the salon if the door into the house is left ajar for a moment.

However, though our cats are deprived of the salon, they live in a house built at a time when plenty of cupboards were considered essential to its comfort. So in almost every room they can explore a cupboard in the hope that it may hold something fresh to sniff. Packing a bag is always a profound interest but that interest is tinged with apprehension. Unpacking a bag provides them with undiluted pleasure. There are no mice, but five years ago Bluebell saw a mouse and to this day she will occasionally spend an hour sitting in front of the hole, long ago filled up, down which that mouse once escaped from her. The bookshelves which she inspected on the evening when she first arrived still afford her a hiding-place in which to postpone bedtime. Like children the cats all hate going to bed when they think the rest of the family is sitting up. They greatly enjoy visits from the B.B.C. to make tape recordings, and even more the preparations for television.

Pippo disapproves of the telephone and if he is in the room when the bell rings will yowl at it indignantly. On the other hand if he hears the front-door bell ring he will hurry along to see who is at the door.

Mercifully all three of the cats dislike velvet, and so our curtains and some of our chairs and couches are not ripped to pieces. Nor, and I write this after crossing my fingers, have they any wish to rip up our carpets. But the material of the furniture on which they like to lean or sharpen their claws is soon a sad sight. However, a few ruined chairs are a small price to pay for the continuous delight of their company.

Yes, there is no doubt our cats are spoilt, but nobody who is not prepared to spoil cats will get from them the reward they are able to give to those who do spoil them.

I say with Swinburne:

> Stately, kindly, lordly friend,
> Condescend
> Here to sit by me.